The Art of Snowboarding

KICKERS, CARVING, HALFPIPES, AND MORE

The Art of
Snowboarding

KICKERS, CARVING, HALFPIPES, AND MORE

Jim Smith

Ragged Mountain Press

Camden, Maine • New York • Chicago • San Francisco • Lisbon
London • Madrid • Mexico City • Milan • New Delhi • San Juan
Seoul • Singapore • Sydney • Toronto

The McGraw·Hill Companies

1 2 3 4 5 6 7 8 9 DOC DOC 9 8 7

Library of Congress Cataloging-in-Publication Data
Smith, Jim (Jim E.)
 The art of snowboarding : kickers, carving, halfpipes, and more / Jim Smith.
     p. cm.
  Includes index.
   ISBN 0-07-145688-0 (pbk. : alk. paper)
  1. Snowboarding. I. Title.
   GV857.S57.S55 2006
   796.93'9--dc22
                            2006012682
 ISBN-13: 978-0-07145688-3
 ISBN-10: 0-07-145688-0

Questions regarding the content of this book should be addressed to
Ragged Mountain Press
P.O. Box 220
Camden, ME 04843
www.raggedmountainpress.com

Questions regarding the ordering of this book should be addressed to
The McGraw-Hill Companies
Customer Service Department
P.O. Box 547
Blacklick, OH 43004
Retail customers: 1-800-262-4729
Bookstores: 1-800-722-4726

Unless otherwise noted, all photographs by Kurt Olesek; Jim Smith is the rider. Illustrations by Joseph Comeau.

To my dad for our "follow-your-bliss" household.

Contents

ACKNOWLEDGMENTS ix

PREFACE xi

INTRODUCTION: HOW TO USE THIS BOOK 1

    Snowboarding as Art 3

    Simplify 3

    A Word on Safety 4

1 GEAR 7

    Boards 7

    Bindings 12

    Boots 14

2 FUNDAMENTALS: SETUP,
STANCE, AND TURNING 17

    Regular or Goofy? 17

    The Balanced Athletic Stance 19

    Stance Setups 20

    Turns and Carving 26

    The Ollie 34

    Turning Drills 36

3 KICKERS 39

    Kicker Etiquette 39

    Kicker Skills 41

Next Steps on Kickers 45
The Hip Jump 57

4 RAILS 61

Rail Etiquette 61
The Stock Approach 61
Ride-on Flat Rail 62
Ollie-on Flat Box, 50/50 Slide 66
Ollie-on Flat Rail, Boardslide 66
Next Steps on Rails 67

5 WOOD 81

50/50 Slide on a Flat Log 81
Ride the Rainbow 83
The Stump Ollie 83
Picnic Table Slide 84
Next Steps on Wood 85

6 HALFPIPE 95

Pipe Layout 95
Halfpipe Etiquette 97
Halfpipe Progression 99
Next Steps in the Halfpipe 110

7 MORE TRICKS OF THE
TRADE 131

The Momentum Leap 131
The Army Man Walk 132
Buttering 133
Layback Slide 136

8 CROSS-TRAINING 139

Skateboarding 139
Core-Strengthening Exercises 144
Stretching 148

INDEX 151

Acknowledgments

I would like to thank Tim Windell, Dave Dowd, and Tom Nordwall for coaching me and teaching me how to be a good snowboarding coach; Kurt Olesek for believing in the project and for his work ethic; Bud Keene and Bob Aubrey for their contributions to this book; and Max Goodwin for his friendship and contribution to my initial proposal for this project. Thanks to my friends and riding partners Grant Stone, Mike D., Jerry Natale, Christy Rost, Mike Meirick, Joe Srholez, Hanz Koch, Jason Troth, Chip Koning, Jeff Potto, Pat Abramson, Cisco Oldani; my Team Summit kids; and my coaches Josh Moses, Leslie Glen, Justin McCarthy, Lara Munch, and Chris Landry. Also thanks to: Quimbola Man Clothing for my first sponsorship, Rossignol Snowboards, Joe Curtis at ThirtyTwo Boots, Vince Sanders at The Boardroom Colorado, Cory Smith at Smith Optics, Ska Brewing, Pouch at Ogio Bags, Barrett at Nike 6.0, Ragged Mountain Press and my editor Bob Holtzman, Team Summit, and the snowboard coaching community. Not to mention Bad Brains, Soul Fly, Fugazi, and Queens of the Stone Age. Finally, I'd like to thank my loving family: Camille and John, Barr, Mom and Dad, and my lovely Christy Rost. Yeah!

(Rider: Dylan Bidez)

Preface

The first time I ever saw a snowboard I was still a kid, sledding at a local hill. One of my neighbors had been to Utah and bought a wooden Burton Performer, and he was out on the hill thrusting and slashing through the powder on either side of our sled track. At the first glimpse I knew snowboarding was for me. I had heard about snowboarding from friends and seen it in magazines and knew that I would try it someday. But when I first saw the ride in action I thought it was beyond cool. It was the coolest cool, the pinnacle of radical, the most fueled, pumped-up thing I had ever witnessed. That Christmas my parents had a snowboard under the tree for me. I was double stoked.

For a few years after that I would always take my board to the local ski area, but the ski area did not allow snowboarding, so I would ski most of the day with my family, then hike a run or a switchback road to satiate my real downhill desire. Those afternoon solo sessions would often last until it was too dark to continue. Berthoud Pass, Colorado, was the only place I could get on a chairlift with my board. My sister would take me and my buddy, Grant Stone, up to Berthoud; if we had the money we would buy lift tickets, and if not, my sister would shuttle us up the pass in her Jeep Cherokee. Grant and I met the coolest people up there. We would share the intoxicating fun of riding through the trees before piling back into the Jeep and laughing all the way back to the top. My first years in the sport marked me and shaped my identity as a lifetime snowboarder. Snowboarding was so fresh and unbounded, my senses were ignited to a new level, and when I rode I was completely immersed in thrill and exhilaration. Every day I would discover new ways to ride, new tricks to try, and new lines to master. I loved skiing and I loved skateboarding, but the freedom I felt in the snowboard ride was unsurpassed; it resonated to my bones. It wasn't only the ride that was so appealing, but also the people I met: a tight-knit tribe of forward movers, alternative thinkers, and crazy humans.

The snowboarding movement continued and soon snowboards were accepted at the resorts. I could now ride the lift instead of hiking a nearby pitch or pirating a run at the ski area. At the same time, snowboard technology was advancing in leaps and bounds. I got hold of a Winterstick snowboard with metal edges and it was a whole new ride. The ability to hold an edge on hard-packed snow opened insane new doors of power and exhilaration. The Rocky Mountain Snowboard Series started up and riders from all over were coming together to session rough, pushed-up halfpipes. The progression was insane. Riders like Andy Hetzel, Dave Dowd, Tim Windell, Kevin Delany, and Butch Bendell blew my mind with the airs they were pulling. I was fifteen and wanted to be like these guys—but in my own way, with my own style.

At this point, snowboarding was absolutely unstoppable. Regional contests grew to national contests, and the nationals grew to worlds, and soon people were handling 10-foot airs out of the halfpipe. The boards were becoming more and more sophisticated, too. So much so that board innovations began to influence the ski designs—quite a switch from just a couple years before. During this time I witnessed an eruption in snowboarding sickness: so many new tricks, new styles, movements, features, and *people*—the coolest people on earth. Before long there was the "pipe dragon"—a machine to cut halfpipes. It cut walls that were consistent from top to bottom, and riders no longer had to show up two days early to shape the pipe they planned to session. It was an amazing transition—the height of freestyle snowboarding—and riding that dragon pipe was so super-fun.

But this book isn't a history of snowboarding. I can't claim to be a true snowboarding pioneer or a historian, just someone who grew up immersed in the ride with a burning desire that kept me up nights for years and years: the desire to get better.

Twenty years later I still love the sport as much as I did then, and for the same reason: Snowboarding remains new and dynamic and progressive, inspiring, fresh, unbounded—limitless. Even within the last two or three years insane changes have continued. A few years ago I could enter a snowboard park and hit a few rails, a 10- or 20-foot tabletop jump, and a dragon-cut 8-foot transition pipe. Now I enter a modern snowboarding park and find the grandest set of hulking monstrosities just waiting to be slayed. The line of big kickers in the most-progressive snowboarding parks might take you over a 30-foot table, then a 40-foot table, and then a 60-foot table! The rail features look like dragons or giant coffins or question marks. The halfpipe has morphed into the super pipe, with 20-foot transitions and a colossal roll-in deck. The budding sport that drew me in as a thrill-seeking kid just keeps on budding, and that keeps me coming back for more. The progression I witnessed years ago is still occurring, but at an elevated level.

I have shaped myself into a snowboarder through all this, and now my personal progression comes mostly from helping other people progress, which is just as fulfilling. This book is my attempt to share the same thrills, relationships, and pure fun with anyone who has the desire to ride.

≈ ≈ ≈

Individuality and personal style are the essence of snowboarding. Each rider sees the terrain differently and chooses his or her own line. Each rider is drawn to riding for his or her own reasons. Nevertheless, in my twenty-plus years as a snowboarder I have observed a few common elements in all the riders I've met.

One common thread is the desire to get better. Everyone on a board, whether on a bunny hill or an Alaskan peak or a 70-foot tabletop jump, wants to improve. They are looking for that next step, and when they reach that step, it is so thrilling and so fulfilling that the *next* next step becomes the next goal. Call it a healthy addiction. To finally succeed at the trick you have been attempting, or make the perfect lockup into a heelside carve, is so rewarding. This book lays out a loose path to all those next steps in turning, jumping, pipe riding, rail riding, and log riding. So take that step.

Snowboarding is not to be super-regimented and overanalyzed. Snowboarding is a sport, but also an art, and it needs to be self-directed and as individual as possible. There is no "best" way to ride and there are no rules for advancement—or enjoyment. The lessons that follow are meant to be a loose guide to put you on a path toward better riding, advanced understanding, and enhanced enjoyment. But they're not the final word. Take what I say into consideration—add it to everything else you have been told by other riders or have heard, read, and experienced—and form your own angle on the super-sweet art of snowboarding.

How to Use This Book

The Art of Snowboarding will help riders of all ages and abilities improve their turning skills and terrain park and halfpipe riding. Designed to be like a slide show in book form, *The Art of Snowboarding* presents each skill or maneuver in simplified core sequences of photos, accompanied by just enough text to explain what you're looking at and what to strive for. The photos reveal the dynamic beauty, amazing athleticism, and appealing aesthetic of snowboarding.

Each skills-related chapter addresses a different discipline. The beginning of the chapter covers the basics of the discipline; the middle is a logical advancement from the basics to more challenging skills; and the final part presents avenues for pushing your limits and developing your own personal style. I call this development *progression* or *progressive snowboarding*, and this concept represents the core of my teaching philosophy. Master the basics, hone the skills, and use your creativity to make each move your own. You will learn by seeing the motions and movements of ripping snowboarders laid out in photo sequences and single shots accompanied by easy explanations. Each skills chapter also includes safety and etiquette tips.

The skills explained here are designed as a guide to set you on the path to better riding, but this is not a book of right and wrong. Use the images and explanations as a template for your own creativity. There is so much happening in the sport of snowboarding today that it is easy to get lost. Even as a snowboarding veteran, I can't believe what I see at the local resorts: jumps bigger than houses, halfpipes the size of fallen hotels, rails in the shape of dragons. It can all be a bit baffling and intimidating. This book gives you a path to killing those dragon-rails, climbing the hotels, and clearing the houses.

Age is not an impediment: No matter how young or old you are, you can do this stuff. I have coached riders from seven to seventy—no exaggeration—and seen people at every age make progress. Take direction from the book. Do the progressions from start to finish. Closely follow the photo demonstrations and the accompanying text and you will be

(Rider: Jake Black)

on the path to any goal you set for yourself. Remember not to rush; be patient and master all the steps one by one. Be realistic—you can't go directly from a 10-foot air to a 60-foot air without hurting yourself. You need to master the 10-footer and get it down, then go for a 15-footer and do that 100 times and get that down, and continue to progress in reasonable increments. I tell my athletes that they have to climb the ladder. I make them do one skill at a time and it builds them into super-strong, all-around good snowboarders.

Pay extra attention to the fundamentals in Chapter 2, because snowboarding starts with how you stand on your board and revolves around the ability to make good turns. Check out the drills at the end of Chapter 2: These *will* make you a better snowboarder. Build your riding on a strong foundation of turning skills. Do all the steps I have laid out in a systematic way and you will stay healthy and uninjured and will be so forking stoked to take the next steps.

SNOWBOARDING AS ART

From one season to the next I see both small changes and bold changes in the riders I coach. I love the new features they ride and I love what I see. I am seeing the forward movement of the coolest sport there is. Daily I witness new variations on snowboarding tricks and variations on the style in which the tricks are executed. These adaptations in style and on-hill features spell progress. Each day you ride you can get better in some way. Strive for progress every day you go out.

Snowboarding fits no mold and is constantly defining and redefining itself. There is just nothing like it. When you do it and do it right, you are doing it like no one else: It's purely individual—an art form as much as a sport. Whether you're on the green run or the biggest terrain park going, you paint your own picture on every descent.

SIMPLIFY

Don't overthink the skills explained in the book. I have tried to keep the explanations simple, concise, and not super-serious. I'm no drill sergeant. You will find a lot of repetition in the explanations; that's because snowboarding revolves around a handful of basic elements. This simplicity is one reason why snowboarding is such a beautiful thing.

Some people break snowboarding down and down and down and overanalyze it and tear it to pieces. Snowboarding doesn't need this, and neither do you. You will learn not by remembering a thousand little rules, but by emulating someone who is good. I think I'm a good teacher, so follow the photo sequences, get the basics down, and then put a bit of a personal spin on it. You only have two edges to worry about. Take advantage of the simplicity.

When I asked Dylan Bidez, one of the young riders I coach, "What do you think about when you ride?" he thought for a second and answered, "Nothing"—and he meant it. That is so pure! To me, that is the ultimate goal. Dylan's body is trained so that riding has become like walking down the street—something that requires no thought while you do it with perfect confidence and smoothness.

I don't expect you to think about absolutely nothing, like a white wall, while you ride—but just don't think about *everything*. All those thoughts in your head will tense you up and freak you out. If you are approaching a rail, you don't need to be thinking, "Bend my legs, keep my eyes up, get my hands out away from my body, point it straight at the rail, load up the tail for my ollie." Relax. All of those approach things fit into one thing called your stance, which I introduce in Chapter 2. So get in your stance and go. Let all the stance elements be one thing and focus on the one key maneuver you are trying to execute. When I ride a rail I have only one thought in my head and that is "Look to the end." I approach the rail relaxed and in my stance, and then I drive onto the rail and look to the end, staying relaxed. In my explanations you will find key phrases like "Look to the end" for rails and log slides, "Look past the lip" for the halfpipe, and "Knees up in the air" for kickers. Check it out, because it works.

A WORD ON SAFETY

Safety is one reason I feel there is a need for this book. I have seen too many injuries that could easily have been avoided. Snowboarding has inherent risks, and you have to expect some bumps and bruises, but with proper attention to safety you can avoid broken bones and other serious injuries that might put you out of commission for a season or more.

A good starting point for safety is fitness for injury prevention. The most common snowboarding injuries are sprained and broken wrists or hands. Check out the hand- and wrist-strengthening techniques in Chapter 8 and practice them. If you are looking to become a hard-charging snowboarder, get your body prepared by being physically active. Ride bikes, hike mountains, run, walk, skateboard, do circuits in the gym, play sports, do the exercises that I demonstrate—just be active every day. If you sit at a desk all week and do nothing but watch screens every night, you'll almost certainly hurt yourself when you push your body on weekends.

Gearing up is another important aspect of safety. Anytime you are riding hard or pushing your limits, you should wear a helmet, as I require of all the kids I coach. (In most of the photo sequences I am not wearing a helmet, but these tricks are all well within my comfort range and were performed under controlled conditions.) Wrist guards, which you wear under your gloves, can help prevent breaks and sprains. Butt and hip pads, which are worn under your snowboarding pants like an extra layer of underwear, aren't so much to avoid serious injuries as to soften the blows and maybe save you some bruises. All of this gear is available at snowboarding shops. Buy it and use it.

Know your limits. Progress slowly and patiently. Master new techniques one by one and you will stay reasonably safe and healthy. When you do bang yourself up, I highly recommend ice packs. I use them frequently.

I have organized this book with your health and safety in mind. Follow these progressions systematically and you will considerably reduce your risk of injury.

CHAPTER 1

Gear

Good gear can make all the difference in a snowboarder's ride. There's nothing like the feeling of a fresh board's glide across the snow on a good day. When you have your gear dialed in, your board becomes an extension of your body.

When choosing gear, the simple rule of "you get what you pay for" usually applies. If you find your board at a chain-style sporting goods store for a really low price, you are probably getting a cheap board that's gonna fall apart or lose its life quickly. I recommend shopping at specialty snowboarding shops. Find a shop you trust with people you relate to and like. Spend a long time choosing your gear: Be deliberate; don't be in a hurry. Pick the brains of the shop owner and workers to find the right gear for your riding style and needs.

A fantastic place to start your research is the product test articles in magazines like *TransWorld Snowboarding*, *Snowboard Magazine*, and *Snowboarder*, and on their websites (www.transworldsnowboarding.com; www.snowboard-mag.com; www.snowboardermag.com).

Another great way to select gear is to go to an "on-snow demo"—a demonstration session where several snowboard vendors have their line of gear for you to try out, usually for free. You can find information about on-snow demos on the websites of ski areas and snowboard manufacturers. The bigger snowboard manufacturers usually have a "demo" van that tours resorts all over the country throughout the snowboarding season.

BOARDS

There are many breeds of snowboard out there on the shelves, all with common design features, and they are all sweet. But for the purpose of this book I will be focusing solely on *freestyle* boards.

First, let's look at some design elements that are key to the performance of every board.

(1) effective edge or running length; (2) tip kick; (3) camber; and (4) tail kick

Design elements of a snowboard.

Camber is the upward curve of the bottom of your board, seen from the side. Lay your board flat on a table and you will see the curve of its base. Camber gives a snowboard life and liveliness when turning.

The *sidecut* is the board's hourglass shape as seen from above. Looking at it from another direction, if you place your board on its edge on a flat surface, you will see its sidecut—where the middle of the board is narrower than the ends. The sidecut is a portion of a big circle, and when you tilt your board on its edge, the path the board takes is along that circle. A deeper sidecut will produce a tighter-radius turn, and a shallower sidecut will produce a larger-radius turn.

A deep sidecut results in a very "edgy" board that will deal you a painful hand if you are off your game for an instant. A mellower sidecut will grant you some forgiveness if you get a little lazy with your riding. Boards designed specifically for rails and kickers usually have a mellower sidecut. Pipe boards usually have a deeper sidecut to rail up the icy pipe walls. When you are shopping for a board, look for one that suits your style of riding.

Camber and sidecut work together, especially in the apex of a turn, when momentum forces your weight down hard on the board. The board's camber reverses: The middle section flexes down, so that the sidecut bites more deeply into the snow, accentuating your turn. As you come out of the apex and some of your momentum comes off the board, the camber springs you back up.

Snowboards come in a range of lengths, and choosing the right length is mainly a function of your height and the type of riding you plan to do. Standing on end, a freestyle board should come up to between your throat and your nose. For rail and wood riding, go a little shorter, and for halfpipe and other higher-speed riding, go a little longer. For a versatile, do-everything board, go with a length that comes up to about your chin. I know this sounds super-simple, but that's how you should keep it.

The width of your ride is mostly relative to the size of your feet. If you got huge feet you are gonna need a wide board. If you have small feet you are gonna want a narrower board. Board manufacturers have this in mind and have designs to fit your needs. Your board

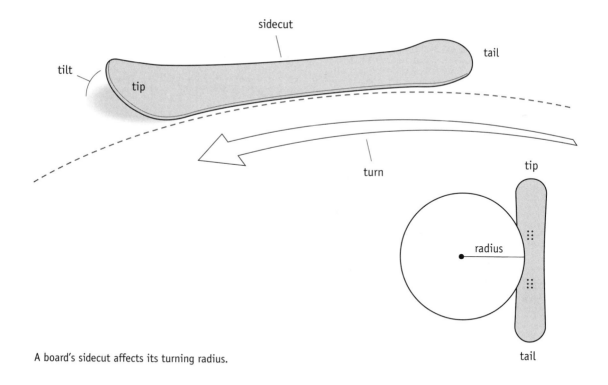

A board's sidecut affects its turning radius.

should be a few centimeters narrower than the length of your feet so that your toe and heel hang over the edges a bit when your foot is in place on the board. If the board is too wide it will be sluggish and slow to respond from edge to edge. If the board is too narrow, your heels and toes will drag in the snow and mess up your turns. Manufacturers also have this in mind and have developed toe and heel ramps to keep your toe and heel overhang up off the snow (see "Bindings" below).

The amount of *flex* in your board is an important consideration. Snowboards come in soft, medium, and stiff. Flex is determined by the stiffness of its core, and it's easy to get a feel for a snowboard's flexibility right in the shop. Hold a board vertically with its tail on the ground. Grab the tip with one hand and push in on the middle, at the highest point of the camber. You'll be able to feel the flex.

A stiff board offers a rider a lot of power and stability in turns and airs, but to get a stiff board to do what it is designed to do, you have to be going fast and riding hard. Stiff boards are also designed for heavier riders. A stiff board offers a less forgiving ride, meaning that you have to be on top of your game to control it; if you get lazy, it will easily catch an edge and slap you onto the snow in a heartbeat. Riders who demand performance—the ones getting big airs out of the pipe, jumping the biggest jumps in the terrain park, and

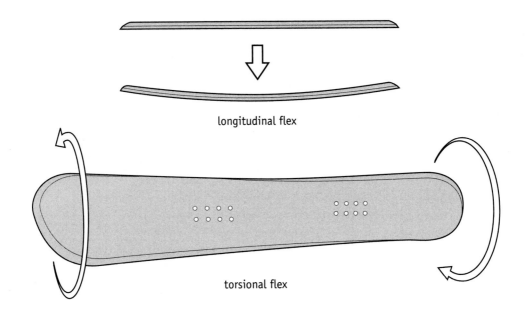

longitudinal flex

torsional flex

Types of board flex.

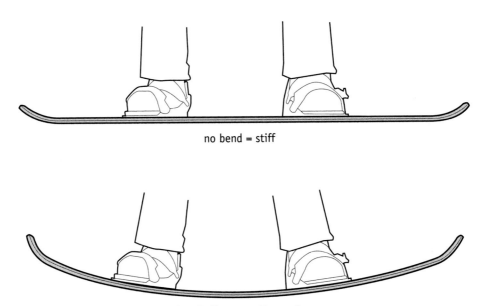

no bend = stiff

bends like a noodle = soft

What's the right amount of flex?

riding steeper terrain at higher speed—usually ride stiff boards.

Medium flex offers a more forgiving ride. You can be traveling at slower speeds and riding a bit mellower, and your medium-flex board will ride well. Medium flex offers great versatility if you want to ride all kinds of terrain, from groomed runs to rails and jumps to halfpipes.

A soft-flex board offers a very forgiving ride and is usually designed for a beginner-level rider. A soft board lacks performance and won't hold up to a hard-charging rider. There is one exception to this, however. Soft boards are sometimes used by skilled riders specifically to ride rails and wood and other varied jibs (stumps, tables, trash cans, or whatever else comes into your path).

Don't just choose a stiff board because it offers the most performance. Remember, it also demands a higher level of skill. Think carefully about your current ability and how you plan to ride, and choose accordingly. You can always get a stiffer board later as your skills progress—and if your riding takes you in that direction.

Despite all these variables in snowboard design, there are just two basic types of freestyle boards: the *directional board* and the *twin-tip board*. Directional boards have a front end (known as

Decoy (twin-tip) board.
(Courtesy Rossignol)

Premier 157 (directional) board.
(Courtesy Rossignol)

the *nose or tip*) and a back end (the *tail*) and are designed to be used mostly in one direction. Twin-tip boards are symmetrical, offering identical performance either way.

The sidecut on a directional board is closer to the tail than the nose, and the tail is a bit stiffer than the tip. The stiff tail provides extra power to pop you from edge to edge in turns. When you're preparing to pop an ollie off the snow, you get more lift by loading the tail—putting more weight on your rear foot to get extra spring from the board. Directional boards offer great versatility to ride different terrain—you can go from a groomed run, into the powdery snow, and among the trees, then into the pipe and terrain park, and have a good all-around ride.

The sidecut on a twin-tip board is centered front-to-rear. The tip and tail are the same length and have the same flex or stiffness. Twin-tip boards are for riders who ride switch (opposite their normal stance) a good amount of the time. A twin-tip board is freestyle-specific, designed to ride on jumps, in the pipe, and on rails; it does not ride trees or powder as well as a directional one. But there's no rule that says you have to follow the rules: I know some riders who are completely "ambidextrous," and they love to ride twin-tip boards on all terrain.

There are hundreds of variations in board design and construction, and since the technology is changing all the time, your best sources of up-to-date information are snowboarding magazines and your local dealer. But understanding these basic issues will get you started in the right direction.

Ideally, when you are in the market for a new board, you should ride a bunch of different boards and find what works for you. (The next chapter shows some examples of different riders' choices. You can take some cues from these good riders.)

BINDINGS

The technology of the *strap*, or *conventional*, *binding* has progressed in leaps and bounds, and there are some great models to choose from. Don't skimp on your binding purchase, because bindings are super-important—they link you to your board.

Freestyle bindings come in stiff, medium, and soft. Riders who need high performance and want immediate response from the board need stiff bindings. Riders who like a little more forgiveness and the ability to make contorted grabs prefer medium or soft bindings.

Modern freestyle bindings come with a bunch of adjustment features so you can customize their feel and fit them to your boots. Bindings also come in small, medium, and large sizes. Check with your shop to be sure you get the size that best fits your boots.

On the back of modern bindings you will find a forward lean adjuster. *Forward lean* on your binding tilts the highback of the binding forward, forcing you to bend your knees.

forward lean
adjustment

toe
ramp

highback
lateral
adjustment

heel ramp

heel cup adjustment

Conventional, medium-stiffness freestyle binding. (Photo courtesy Rossignol)

With no forward lean, your highback will be set bolt upright at 90 degrees. The increments of adjustment usually come in clicks of 1 degree, but this varies with different brands of bindings. Start by giving yourself only one or two clicks. Big forward lean offers you big power on heelside turns. Experiment with different forward-lean settings and give each trial a real chance. If you are scrubbing out in your turns or having a hard time getting low in your stance, the remedy could be as simple as turning the dial.

The heel cup adjustment is crucial to riders with bigger feet. Your feet must be centered across the board, edge-to-edge. You can't ride well if your toes are hanging way out over your toe edge while your heels are well inside your heel edge. Mounting screws that hold the heel cup in place are located on the sides of the back of the binding's base plate. Loosening these screws will allow you to slide your heel cup forward and back. Most modern bindings have increments marked on the binding for the size of your boot. So if you wear a size 10 boot, set your heel cup at the 10 mark. Try it—you'll like it.

Most modern bindings also have ramp-shaped plates that sit over the mounting disks. These toe and heel ramps raise your boot up so your heels and toes don't drag in the snow when you tilt your board up into a carve. The additional height also gives you more leverage to get up on your edges. Adjust your toe and heel ramps to sit within, or *just* over, the board's edges.

Bindings typically have an additional adjustment that moves the highback laterally—in other words, it moves from side to side in the heel cup. (This is separate from the angular adjustment of the mounting disks on your bindings' base plates, which is described in the next chapter.) This adjustment is used primarily on your lead foot. By tweaking your highback more toward the nose of the board, you will be able to apply pressure more directly to your edge on a heelside turn. The more angle you have on your bindings, the more you need to turn your highbacks to be parallel to your heel edge.

For more on binding adjustments, see the discussion of stance in the next chapter.

BOOTS

Boots are another crucial part of your snowboarding gear; they provide ankle support, connect you to the bindings, and allow you to transfer your body's movements to the board. Modern snowboarding boots are designed for performance and comfort. As long

Soft-medium flex freestyle boot with boa lace system. (Courtesy Rossignol)

Medium-stiff flex freestyle boot. (Courtesy Rossignol)

as you take your time selecting your boots, you don't need to sacrifice either of these elements.

As with boards and bindings, freestyle boots come in stiff, medium, and soft. A stiff boot offers performance and a great deal of support to your ankles, but lacks tweakability and "feel" for the terrain. A medium-flex boot offers a better feel for the terrain and a bit more tweakability, but less ankle support. A soft boot has little ankle support and lacks "performance," but you can tweak the hell out of your tricks. But because of the lack of ankle support, I do not recommend a super-soft boot.

Choose a boot to suit your riding style. Different boots come with different bells and whistles—many of these are gimmicks, but others are worthwhile features, and the difference between the two is very much a matter of opinion. When you are trying on boots in your local shop, take your time. Walk around the shop, strap yourself into a board with the boots on, and pick the shop worker's brain on what he or she suggests.

CHAPTER 2

Fundamentals:
Setup, Stance, and Turning

The setup of your bindings, your stance, and turning skills form the very foundation of snowboarding. Your binding setup greatly influences your riding style, and your stance is critical to your ability to turn. Whether you aim to become a free-carve rider, a park and pipe master, a rail rider, or an Alaskan first-descent kingpin, you must master these fundamentals.

In this chapter, you'll learn the *balanced athletic stance*. I'll refer to this frequently, so let's get it right from the start. You will also learn how to set up the bindings on your board to suit your riding style, and you'll see examples of different riders' setups.

This chapter also includes a guide to turns. The way you turn is key to your snowboarding progress, so pay attention to these tips, then get out and practice and learn. Not only will you become a better rider, but you'll also discover the sweet sensation of a locked-up, smooth carve. Polished turning skills will make it easier to progress to jumps, rails, and the halfpipe. On the other hand, if you get into bad turning habits early in your riding, it will impair your ability to conquer new challenges. So even if you're already a proficient rider, look closely at the tips in this chapter; you'll find some useful stuff in there.

The end of the chapter will walk you through the *ollie*, which is basically an air popped straight off the snow with the power of your body and your board. The ollie is a foundation skill that you will need to hit jumps, rails, wood features, and the halfpipe.

REGULAR OR GOOFY?

If you snowboard with your left foot forward, you ride *regular*. Right foot forward makes you *goofy-footed*. In spite of some joking by regular-footers to the effect that goofy-foot-

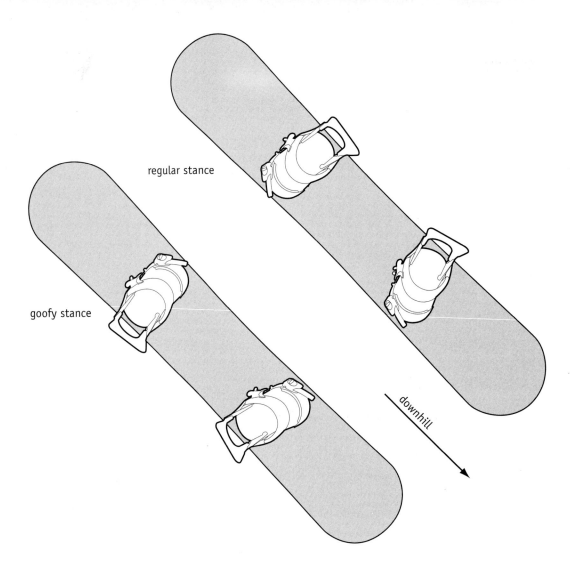

regular stance

goofy stance

downhill

ers are, somehow, goofy, there's absolutely no difference in the methods or the skills involved—it's purely a matter of what feels more natural to you. (A few riders are completely "ambidextrous" and are perfectly comfortable going either way.)

There are a few methods to determine if you're regular or goofy-footed. Try running up to a patch of ice and sliding, and see which foot you place in front. Or, do this same test in your socks on a smooth floor. Or encourage a friend to sneak up behind you someday and give you a shove. Which foot did you lead with to catch your balance?

These methods aren't foolproof, however. The best test is to ride both ways and see which way feels more natural.

THE BALANCED ATHLETIC STANCE

The balanced athletic stance is super-simple. Stand on your board with all your joints bent and relaxed. Bend your ankles forward slightly while keeping your feet flat in your boots. Keep your knees bent and slightly spread out to distribute your weight evenly across the

The balanced athletic stance.

board. This will enable you to get more power out of the board, so pay attention to your knees and try not to tilt them in toward each other. Turn your hips slightly to face downhill. Slightly bend at the waist while keeping your back tall and straight. (Don't bend over with your butt sticking out over your heel edge.) Turn your shoulders downhill in anticipation of what's ahead. I refer to this as "addressing the fall line." (The *fall line* is the steepest direction downhill at any point on the slope. If you drop a ball anywhere on a hill, it will begin to roll down the fall line.) Keep your head high and your eyes up.

STANCE SETUPS

The setup of your bindings will define how you ride. The last thing you want is a wack setup with your feet positioned all weird on your stick. In other words, if your setup is poor, your stance will be off, and that will affect your riding. So here are some guidelines for setting up your stance.

- The distance between the centers of the bindings' mounting disks is the basic *stance measurement*. Your feet should be positioned a few inches wider than your shoulders.

- For an all-around setup that works well for carving on groomed runs, riding pipe, hitting kickers, and cruising in the woods, your stance should be *offset*, or centered a few inches back from the board's center. In other words, your forward foot should be farther from the nose of the board than your back foot is from the tail. Offset is also known as *setback*.

- On the other hand, if you ride *fakie*, or switch a lot, you'll probably prefer to center your stance tip-to-tail. (Switch and fakie mean the same thing: riding your board backwards, or in the opposite direction of your normal, regular- or goofy-footed stance.)

- The mounting disks on your bindings' base plates are marked with degrees of angle. When the disks are set at 0 degrees, your bindings, and therefore your feet, are oriented straight across the board, perpendicular to the long axis. As you rotate the bindings on the disks you will create your *stance angles*. A positive angle means the foot points more toward the tip of the board, and a negative angle means it points toward the tail. Your front foot should have between 15 and 30 degrees of positive angle. (The front foot's angle is never negative.)

- Your rear foot should be between 0 and negative 20 degrees. (Positive angle on the front foot and negative angle on the rear foot, so that the toes point away from each other, is known as a *duck stance*. Positive angle on both feet puts you in a *forward stance*. The forward stance is used by racers and alpine boarders. For the purposes of learning the tricks in this book, it's a good idea to go with the duck stance. Besides, a few degrees of negative angle on your trailing foot will encourage stability in all types of riding.) You should use a great deal of negative angle on your trailing foot only if you do a lot of fakie riding.

I recommend this range of stances for most trick riders, and I suggest you give them a try. But stance is subject to a great deal of opinion and personal preference. A lot of awesome riders—including some of my most talented students—use very different setups. Take a look at the following examples that these riders rock. Also observe the stances of other riders around you. Experiment with different stances to find what works for you.

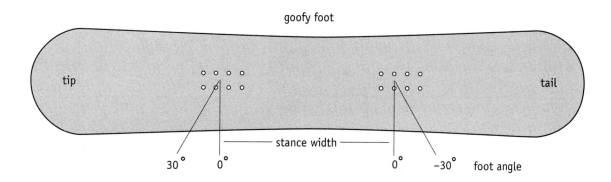

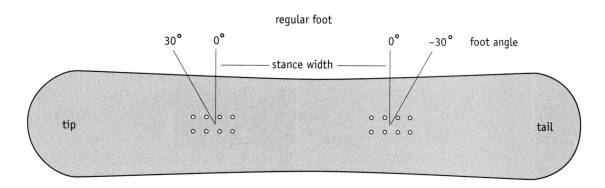

Stance angles.

Jim Smith

Age: 34
Height: 5'11"
Weight: 160 lb.
Specialty: pipe, kickers,
   and freeriding

Setup

  Regular
  Board length: 159 cm
  Stance: 22½"
  Offset: 2"
  Front foot angle: +27
     degrees
  Rear foot angle: −6
     degrees

Clair Bidez

Age: 17
Height: 5'1"
Weight: 110 lb.
Specialty: pipe

Setup

  Regular
  Board length: 150 cm
  Stance: 21"
  Offset: 2"
  Front foot: +18 degrees
  Rear foot: −6 degrees

Andrew "Droid" Steward

Age: 19
Height: 5'11"
Weight: 175 lb.
Specialty: rails, kickers, and
wood

Setup

Regular
Board length: 155 cm
Stance: 25"
Offset: none
Front foot: +15 degrees
Rear foot: −15 degrees

Mike Markowitz

Age: 32
Height: 5'10"
Weight: 180 lb.
Specialty: pipe, kickers,
and freeriding

Setup

Regular
Board length: 159 cm
Stance: 21"
Offset: 2"
Front foot: +27 degrees
Rear foot: −6 degrees

Nick Larson

Age: 15
Height: 6'0"
Weight: 135 lb.
Specialty: pipe and
    freeriding

Setup

Regular
Board length: 155 cm
Stance: 21½"
Offset: 2"
Front foot: +23 degrees
Rear foot: −3 degrees

Dylan Bidez

Age: 14
Height: 5'10"
Weight: 155 lb.
Specialty: pipe, rails, and
    kickers

Setup

Goofy
Board length: 155 cm
Stance: 22½"
Offset: 1"
Front foot: +18 degrees
Rear foot: −12 degrees

Jake Black

Age: 17
Height: 5'9"
Weight: 140 lb.
Specialty: rails, pipe, and
   kickers

Setup

   Goofy
   Board length: 156 cm
   Stance: 22½"
   Offset: none
   Front foot: +27 degrees
   Rear foot: −0 degrees

Jarrett Packer

Age: 31
Height: 6'1"
Weight: 170 lb.
Specialty: kickers, pipe,
   and freeriding

Setup

   Regular
   Board length: 161 cm
   Stance: 22"
   Offset: 2"
   Front foot: +27 degrees
   Rear foot: −12 degrees

Flexion.

TURNS AND CARVING

There is a distinct difference between turning your board and carving it. As a beginner, you learn make turns by sliding and scrubbing your board from edge to edge. As you get better and more comfortable with your edges, you need to graduate from sliding your turns to carving. When you're carving, you are getting the board

Extension.

up on an edge and locking its sidecut into the mountain. Once you're locked in, the shape of the board does a lot of the turning for you. Carving a turn is super rewarding and great fun. This chapter will guide you through it.

There are basically three types of turns in snowboarding—all pretty self-explanatory: short-radius, medium-radius, and large-radius. Each turn has three phases.

1. *Initiation:* building speed, heading into the turn
2. *Apex:* in the heart of the turn, really carving
3. *Completion:* coming out of the turn, building speed again

To execute turns you must understand the three basic elements of a turn:

◆ *Edging:* simply tilting your board up on its edge with your ankles

- *Flexion* and *extension:* bending your knees to get low; and: extending your knees to stand tall again, respectively
- *Rotation:* turning your hips and shoulders to face, or *address*, where you are going

Now let's see how the three elements of a turn are used in the three phases, starting with the short-radius turn.

Short-Radius Turns

In initiating the short-radius turn you shift your weight forward, slightly over your front foot. In the apex of the turn your weight will be centered, and in the completion it will be slightly over your trailing foot and the tail of your board. (Don't overthink this stuff—just let it happen.) Carve the short-radius turn with quick edging movements, using your ankles to engage the toeside edge of the board (by lifting your heels) or the heelside edge (by raising your toes). Popping from edge to edge, going toe to heel and heel to toe between your turns, is known as *edge transfer*.

Your flexion and extension movements should not be super-defined, but rhythmic, snappy, up-and-down movements. Bend down slightly when riding through the apex of the turn; this will drive your weight down over the engaged edge. Then extend when coming out of the apex to take the weight off the board and make your edge transfer.

Your upper body will be rotated to face down the hill, and will remain facing downhill with only a subtle rotation in

Short-radius turns.

your shoulders and hips. Your trailing arm will stay over your trailing leg. Your leading arm will be slightly over your toe edge on your toe-side turn and over your heel edge on your heel-side turn. The short-radius turn is used on steeper terrain to control speed, to maneuver through bumps, and to make quick speed adjustments when approaching a feature such as a big jump, log, or rail. It is also super-fun in the soft snow on the edge of a run. During short-radius turns you should generate a snappy quick rhythm. Bang out the turns: bam, bam, bam. You can really stack them up and make a thousand turns in one run. Good fun.

Medium-Radius Turns

The medium-radius turn is a more opened-up version of the short-radius turn and is executed at higher speed. I will explain the toe-side medium-radius turn first.

Toe-Side

Initiate the toe-side turn by moving your weight forward over your toes and on the ball of your front foot. During the apex of the turn, your weight will be centered over the balls of both feet. In the completion, your weight will be over the tail of your

Medium-radius toe-side turn.

board and the ball of your trailing foot. Your edging movement will be just enough to get your board tilted up onto its sidecut.

In the photo sequence I start the turn standing slightly tall with my knees extended. As I progress through the turn to the apex I flex my knees and break a good deal at the waist, getting low and powerful and driving my weight over the center of my toe edge. At the completion, I extend my knees, getting my weight up off my edge in preparation for my edge transfer and the next turn. Notice that my upper body is rotated in anticipation of the direction of my next turn. My leading arm is up away from my body and out over my toe edge, leading me through the turn. My trailing hand is relaxed, out over my trailing leg. You can give the snow a little brush with your trailing hand on the toe-side turn for fun and a bit of style. This is especially sweet in powder.

Tip: be patient. If you end the turn too quickly scrubbing or sliding may result. You want to carve a trench the whole way through the turn and into the next.

Heel-Side

To flow from the medium-radius toe-side turn to the medium-radius heel-side turn, start by riding tall in your athletic stance with your weight slightly forward and over your leading foot's heel. Tilt your ankles to get your board riding on its heel-side edge. During the apex of the turn transfer your weight back a bit, so that it's equal on both feet, while lifting your toes and driving your heel edge down. Push your knees slightly outward to distribute your weight evenly. At this stage the camber of your board will re-verse, biting into the turn. In the completion of the turn shift your weight over your trailing heel and trailing leg.

Medium-radius heel-side turn.

Your flexion and extension movements should be sharply defined, so that you really drop down in the apex of the turn by bending your knees and breaking at the waist. In this middle stage of the heel-side turn, you want to be in the seated position, as seen in the photo. (The sensation of the seated position is really cool.) Extend up as you come out of the turn in preparation to pop to your next edge. At the end of your extension the camber of your board will pop back into place; allow this popping action to spring you to your next edge. Notice my upper body is rotated down the hill in anticipation of the direction of my next turn; my shoulders are square and horizontal. My leading hand is leading me through the turn held well out over my heel edge. My trailing hand is held relaxed over my trailing leg and away from my body. As you get better at this type of turn you will not be traveling on your flat base at all. You will be popping from edge to edge using your camber, cutting well-defined trenches in the snow as you go.

Large-Radius Turns

Now we're having fun, because the large-radius turn means you are really opening it up and rockin' along at high speed. The large-radius turn mirrors the medium-radius except it is more drawn out.

Toe-Side

As shown in the photo sequence, I initiate the toe-side large-radius turn with my weight slightly forward, standing tallish in my athletic stance (1). As I reach the apex I flex my knees, starting to get low and tilting the board with my ankles onto its edge (3). In the apex I am good and low, with my weight centered over my feet and my board tilted onto its edge and sidecut (5). (My knees are too close together here; try to open up your knees a bit more than this.) In the completion of the turn I extend, and my weight is slightly in the

Large-radius toe-side turn.

"*back seat*" (7 and 8). (Leaning slightly back on the board's tail.) My upper body is facing the way I am headed. Your upper body will face across the fall line at the beginning and end of the large-radius turn. As with the other turns, my hands are up and away from my body. My leading hand and arm lead me through the turn and my trailing arm is held out over my trailing leg. As you get good at this you will not be traveling on your flat base, but will snap from heel-side edge to toe-side edge and back again, carving a clean trench in the snow.

Heel-Side

I initiate the large-radius heel-side turn with my weight slightly forward, standing tall in my athletic stance (1). Reaching the apex of the turn, I tilt my board up on its edge with my ankles, feeling for the lockup of my sidecut (3). I flex my knees to get low and transfer my weight to the center of the board. In the apex I am locked up on my sidecut, with my weight centered and my legs bent, solid in the seated position (4 and 5). As I reach the completion of the turn I transfer my weight to the tail of the board and extend up off

Large-radius heel-side turn.

my edge. My shoulders are square and horizontal (8). My leading hand leads me through the turn out over my heel-side edge. My trailing hand is throwing a shaka (the "hang-loose" sign).

This turn has direct application to pipe riding, which uses many of the same motions. The large-radius turn is also used on wide-open runs and bowls. It's so nice. Feel the acceleration.

THE OLLIE

The *ollie*—an air popped off the snow with only the power of your body and your board—is a key skill for snowboarders. The ollie will help you hit jumps, ride pipe and get onto rails that require an air. You can also use it to pop over any obstacle that may be in your way or just looks fun to ride over.

Start by practicing the ollie at a standstill on a flat surface.

For your first attempts, try the ollie while standing still on a flat spot on the mountain. Start by getting really low, bending your knees and slightly bending your waist (1). Spring out of this low position by transferring your weight over your back foot (2). This movement will *load the tail* (i.e., flex the tail by shifting your weight to the back of the board). When your legs are almost fully extended, allow the flex of the tail of your board to pop you into the air and, at the same time, pull your knees to your chest (3). On your way down, extend your legs in such a way that you land simultaneously on both feet (4).

It's common when learning to ollie that your front foot will come down first, but this is no good. Stomp down with your weight equally distributed over both feet. Bang!

Once you have a feel for the ollie on the flats, try it on a run with a little speed.

TURNING DRILLS

The Slide-into-the-Carve Drill

Beginning riders usually learn to turn by sort of buttering in a sloppy skid from toe to heel and heel to toe, without really getting the board up on its edge. This drill will help you become more aware of your edges and improve your ability to tilt your board onto its edge with your ankles. This will get your board's edges and sidecut working they way there were designed. When it happens, you will feel it.

The drill is simple. Start at a slow to medium speed with a toeside sliding turn utilizing the base of your board more so than its edge. In the middle of your slide (3 and 4), tilt your board abruptly onto its edge with your ankles, and let the edge lock up and take you the way it wants (4). Feel the board's sidecut biting into the snow and taking over the turn. Try it toeside and heelside. This drill will get you carving your turns instead of sliding them.

Slide-into-the-carve drill.

The Rail-Grab Drill

This is one of my favorite turning drills. It was taught to me by my old bro Dave Dowd. The rail-grab drill should be practiced on a wide-open run with a mellow pitch and few people around. You will base the drill on the large-radius turn, trying to traverse across the fall line at the end of each turn. The explanation sounds a little complicated, but take a cue from the photos and I think it will click.

Heel-Side

Pick up a bit of speed and drop into a large-radius heel-side turn. In the apex of the turn get really low, bending your knees and waist. Reach between your feet and grab the toe-side rail (edge) with your trailing hand. Hold on through the apex and completion of the turn and traverse a bit across the fall line, still holding onto that rail. Let go and dive right into a toe-side turn.

Toe-Side

The rail grab on a toe-side turn is harder. With your leading hand reach behind your back and grab your heel-side rail between your feet. Hang on through the entire turn and through a bit of a traverse across the fall line. Keep it up six or eight times and really push yourself with super-hard edging and higher speed until you spin out.

This is a fantastic balance drill and it is super-fun. It will teach you to get low in your turns and will give you an idea of just how low you can get—and getting low is always good. It will also give you an awareness of your edges so that, eventually, your grabs will become second nature.

Rail-grab drill heel-side turn. (Rider: Jarrett Packer)

Rail-grab drill on a toe-side turn.

CHAPTER 3

Kickers

Kickers are an awesome part of snowboarding. These jumps offer you a chance to fly. In no other board sport can you so easily access big air. Surfing friends living the tropical lifestyle on the waves and in the sand tell me that the big air of kickers is something they wish they had in their sport.

Park kickers have recently been taken to new levels of sickness. On any given day you will see humans flying 60 or 70 feet through the air. The sheer size of these kickers, known variously as *booters, jumps, cheese wedges,* or *tables,* is insanely massive. The modern big jumps being built and sessioned resemble my entire condo complex—except that they're fun to jump a snowboard off of. Fortunately, modern park builders also build entry-level kickers.

Park kickers are relatively easy to learn, and this chapter will demonstrate the process in a logical progression. Get out on your local hill and find a small starter jump. Begin by learning the first skill in this chapter and work your way through the skills in order, mastering each step as you go. This format is designed to keep you healthy, safe, and out of the ski patrol room.

KICKER ETIQUETTE

It is a must to scope out a new park before you drop in: Just roll through the park and have a look at all the features. Check out the transitions of the jumps. Check out the landings, and look for holes or chunks of snow that might mess you up. Check out how other riders are handling the jumps: Watch how much speed they use on a jump, and note the lines they choose. Be very careful to stay off the kicker landing area, as you will get hit and seriously injured (or worse).

Once you have the lay of the land, you can head back to the start. At the top of the park or on the drop-in deck for a kicker there will be a loose lineup of riders getting ready

Lining up to drop in.

to drop in. Get into the lineup and shuffle your way to the front. Try not to sit down in the lineup, or you will get passed up (*snaked*) and people won't take you seriously. When you get to the front of the lineup, raise your hand and call out, nice and loud, "Dropping!"

I'll say it again: never stand in the landing of a park jump. If you wipe out in a landing, get up and get out of there as fast as you can. If a rider is hurt and can't get out of the landing, close the jump by placing your board on the lip of the jump, standing on the jump with your arms in an X over your head, and yelling at anyone who tries to come your way. If you're the one who's hurt, get someone to do this for you.

KICKER SKILLS

Roller Airs

The best way to progress into hitting park kickers is to get used to airing over *rollers*—natural bumps in the terrain on a groomed run. Approach the roller nice and low in your athletic stance with your hands out away from your body (1). Flatten out your base and center your weight over your board. As you approach the top of the roller, begin to extend up out of your super-low stance (2), shifting your weight slightly back to load up your tail. At the top of the roller pop your ollie and bring your knees up in the air (3). Extend your legs slightly, anticipating your landing (4), then absorb the landing with your

Roller air.

Continued on next page

legs by flexing/bending your knees. Stomp your board down, landing solid with your weight centered (5).

Tip: It is important to pop your air off of your flat base. Refer to Chapter 2 to become familiar with loading your tail to pop into your ollie.

The Rollover

Once you're comfortable getting air on rollers, it's time to step up to true kickers. We're going to take it in slow stages. Before really going for air, we are first going to simply ride over the jump to get the feel of the transition and landing.

Find a good small jump to start out on. Sideslip down the drop-in deck, then point your board straight at the kicker. Get low in your athletic stance and flatten out your base. Ride up the transition, staying low, and roll on over the lip and the backside of the jump. You may get a tiny bit of air, but try to stay on the ground. Keep your base flat and ride on down the landing. This step is just to get the feel of riding in your low stance and flattening out your base. It is also very important to feel the transition of the jump and the transition of the landing. Feel it.

Rollover.

The Momentum Air

Now that you feel comfortable with the jump's transitions, it's time to hit the thing with a bit of speed. For this step you will get in your low stance and simply stay there as you go over the jump. The momentum you are carrying will send you through the air.

Momentum air.

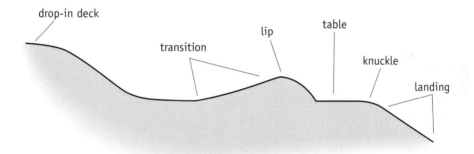

Anatomy of a kicker.

Have a look at the speed other riders are carrying to the jump, and get into position above the jump to carry about the same amount of speed. Drop in nice and low in your stance with your base flat on the snow. As you reach the lip, simply stay in your low, solid athletic stance and let your momentum and the jump send you into the air. Do not try and force yourself into the air with an ollie: Just flow off the lip and stay in your stance.

In the air, stay loose but solid in your stance. Stomp the landing down with both feet. Keep your head up and look down the landing. Keep your board pointed down the landing and ride it out.

Tip: You only want to be a few feet in the air for this step and to land on the table or the knuckle; it's OK to not make it to the downhill part of the landing.

Add the Ollie

Time to go bigger, buddy. For this step you are going to combine your momentum with the power of an ollie. You are now gonna clear the tabletop of the jump and make the landing for a real-deal kicker air.

Approach the jump with a bit more speed than in the momentum air step. Get low in your stance with your arms up away from your body. Keep your base flat on the snow with your weight centered. As you reach the lip, shift your weight back slightly to load your tail. When your tip reaches the lip, pop an ollie off your tail into the air. Bring your knees up and keep facing downhill, looking to the landing. Stay centered over your board in the air. Anticipate your landing by extending your legs slightly. Stomp that landing down, absorbing it with your knees and keeping your weight centered.

Tip: The movements in this step are the same as in the roller air step. If you are having trouble keeping your base flat on the approach or staying centered in the air, go back to the groomed run and do some more roller airs to become comfortable and confident with these motions.

Adding an ollie.

Get the Grab

Indy air.

To taste the true sweetness of the kicker air you now must *get the grab*! Your approach will be the same, low and centered in your stance. Keep that base nice and flat. As you reach the lip, pop into the air and bring your knees up. If you have your knees nice and high, your trailing hand will be right there to grab the toe-side rail between your feet for a nice *indy air*. So grab it and hold the grab solid in the air. You must completely close your hand on the rail. (Slapping or tickling your rail is a good try but doesn't count.)

Keep your eyes up, looking to your landing; don't look down at your grab. In anticipation of your landing, let go of the rail and slightly extend your legs. Stomp it down solid and centered, sucking the landing up with your knees, and ride it out.

Tip: Don't force these movements. Your approach, pop, air, grab, and landing should all flow smoothly. If you are fighting any of these motions, take one or two steps back and master those motions before moving forward again.

NEXT STEPS ON KICKERS

Here's a field guide to the basic grabs you will see going down on your local kickers. Check out these riders and their styles, and then go out and shape your own style.

Tail Grab

For the tail grab, your trailing hand grabs the tip of your tail.

(Rider: Jake Black)

(Rider: Jason Troth)

(Rider: Andrew "Droid" Steward)

Indy Air

Here, you reach between your feet and grab the toe-side edge with your trailing hand.

(Rider: Andrew "Droid" Steward)

(Rider: Jake Black)

Stale Fish

Use your trailing hand to grab the heel edge between your feet.

(Rider: Robert Borchardt)

(Rider: Jake Black)

Mute Air

Use your leading hand to grab the toe edge between your feet.

(Rider: Jake Black)

(Rider: Harry Kerney)

Method Air

Use your leading hand to grab the heel edge between your feet.

(Rider: Joe Otremba)

(Rider: Andrew "Droid" Steward)

(Rider: Rachel Nelson)

More Grabs

Crail air.

Switch indy.

THE HIP JUMP

Hip jump. For a regular footer, this would be a "backside" hip.

A *hip* is a kicker feature with a normal downhill takeoff and lip but a side landing. You approach a hip as you do a regular jump, but you land on the side of the hip.

On your first few attempts at a hip, just roll over it to get the feel of the transition, the speed, and the motion of turning your board slightly for your landing. After you're comfortable with that, go for some air.

Approach the hip at a little bit of an angle in anticipation of the side landing. Aim your board for the corner of the jump that will send you toward the landing. Pop your air and turn your hips and shoulders to square up for the landing. Get your knees up in the air and grab method/backside (leading hand on the heel-side edge between your feet, and hold the grab. Let go of your rail and extend your legs for the landing. Stomp the base flat on the landing, absorb the impact with your knees, and ride it out centered over your board. Hip jumps are killer!

Hip Styles

Here are some different grabs you can try over hips. Check out the style of these riders, take inspiration, and go do it with your own style.

Crail air backside hip.

Frontside air frontside hip. (Rider: Mike Markowitz)

Lien air frontside hip.

Method air backside hip. (Rider: Adam Merriman)

(Rider: Kyle McCafferty)

CHAPTER 4

Rails

One of your snowboard's coolest attributes is its ability to ride on and conquer all kinds of materials—not just snow, but wood and metal as well. The aesthetic of the rail slide is super cool, and the ring of the rail in your ears when you bang on it stokes your senses. When you clean the rail from start to finish, it's thrilling and rewarding, and it will keep you sessioning and pushing your skills all day long. The rail slide has become a cornerstone of modern riding for one bottom-line reason: fun.

You will find a plethora of rail features in most terrain parks. The rails can be intimidating, but if you stay calm, relax, and start on mellow features, you will minimize the risk. Find a small *ride-on* box (where the uphill end is flush with the snow so you don't have to do an ollie to get up), or flat rail and follow the progressions in this chapter. Soon you will be progressing through a whole new field of fun on your jib stick. Check it out, get stoked, and step up to the rails!

RAIL ETIQUETTE

When you're ready to roll up to a rail feature, be aware of the riders around you. Notice who's taking more speed at the feature, and how high people are starting on the hill. When you are ready to drop, be assertive and stand up. Get in the lineup, shuffle forward, and when you are at the front call, "Dropping in!" with your hand up. You can also call "Next drop!" when you want to be next.

THE STOCK APPROACH

Approach the feature by sideslipping down the run-in. Stop 10 or 15 feet above the feature and get into your athletic stance. When you are ready, point your board directly at the feature. Address the feature with your body facing toward the rail, your leading hand

Guerilla Rail-Bashers

My first memorable experience of snowboarding on rails was in 1992 on Loveland Pass, Colorado, while filming for a snowboarding video called *The Hard, the Hungry and the Homeless.* The crew and I had been sessioning some powder, and on the way home someone spotted a half-buried metal road gate in front of a Department of Transportation maintenance building. Being the scavengers we were, we proceeded to set up the gate as a rail slide, then sessioned the hell out of it for hours, and came back for more on several subsequent days. We ended up bending it, scratching the paint, and, in the end, breaking it off its hinges. This practice was totally guerilla, which was in keeping with our "seek and destroy" attitude of the time. We weren't really out to slide a rail that day or even trying to be the best guy out there sliding it. It was more just an impulse thing—"because it was there." The video we were shooting really spoke the truth, because we *were*, by and large, hard, hungry, and homeless. Since then I think I've matured a bit, and I have more respect for others' property, both private and public. In retrospect, it was thoroughly irresponsible, I wouldn't do it again, and I urge you not to either . . . but it *was* awesome fun!

Anyway, that 10-foot-long green metal gate at the bottom of Loveland Pass was the height of snowboarding progression in '92, and sessions like that one paved the way for resorts around the world to build a plethora of on-hill rail features. This evolution is a real bonus, because today you don't have to be a delinquent to kill the rails.

Approaching a rail.

over the heelside edge or the tip of your board, and your head up. Stay centered. Stay committed. Stay straight on target— no turns! Be powerful. This approach will apply to almost all rail features. Avoid the common mistake of making quick adjustments and turns all the way up to the start of the rail. All those last-minute motions have a tendency to mess you up. So get lined up and go!

RIDE-ON FLAT RAIL
50/50 SLIDE

Find a mellow ride-on rail and check it out carefully. Scope out the pitch (steepness) and texture of the run-in and the feature itself. Check out other people who are hitting it and how fast they are going at it. Try to learn from their successes and mistakes.

The *50/50 position* refers to your board being balanced the long way on the rail. Point your board down the approach straight at the rail. Power onto the rail with a small

Ride-on flat rail, 50/50 slide.

wheelie-like motion. Stay centered over your board with your weight forward, looking to the end of the rail. Power off the rail with another popping motion and ride out the landing.

Tip: Power on and power off *all* rail-style features. If you slide off the side you need to pop yourself off, not just fall off. Make it happen; don't let it happen to you.

50/50 Flash to Boardslide

Drive onto the rail with a subtle ollie motion. Stay centered and forward on your board, with your head up and looking to the end of the rail. Near the middle or end of the rail, when you feel locked onto the rail in the 50/50 position, "flash" yourself into the *boardslide position* by pushing your trailing foot and leg out to the side, so that the board is cross-wise on the rail. Turning your hips and shoulders to face the direction you're traveling will help you get into the boardslide position. You gotta stay centered over the rail and over your board, while leaning forward slightly and looking to the end of the rail and the landing. At the end of the slide snap your trailing foot, shoulders, and hips back into your athletic stance, and land with your board pointing down the hill. Ride it out. Hike it and do it again!

Ride-on flat rail, 50/50 flash to boardslide.

Tip: During your first few attempts at this trick your board should only turn about 45 degrees, not the full 90. As you get more comfortable, flash harder and get totally sideways on the thing. You can also try this flash motion on the flat groomed trail to get the feel of snapping your board sideways and snapping it back into position.

Rail Practice Drills

To practice sliding rails, you can visualize and simulate rail moves on a flat groomed run. This type of training reduces your risk and builds confidence.

Find a flat area and take yourself through the motions of sliding a rail. You can become more comfortable snapping your board sideways into boardslide position and snapping it back into landing position. Try different body positions and find out what works best. Work at keeping your hands out in front of you and your elbows over your knees, and tune in on where you have more or less pressure on your edge. In both the frontside and regular boardslide positions, your edge pressure needs to be slightly stronger on your uphill edge or totally centered, so you don't catch your downhill edge on the rail or box.

Find out where your hands and arms are most comfortable. Some riders like their hands and arms up at shoulder level, and some like their hands and arms low, way down by their knees.

To take these groomed-run drills a step further, you can put a line in the snow to represent the rail, or find a bamboo pole to act as your rail. Just lay the pole on the snow and ride it. You could also set up your own *rails* right in your yard, using old pipe or even two-by-four boards. Remember, there is no set rule on how you should ride a rail. Snowboarding allows individual expression. The more you make it your own, the better it feels. Slide on.

50/50 Flash to Frontside Boardslide

Ride-on flat rail, 50/50 flash to frontside boardslide.

Frontside is a little confusing here, 'cause you're actually gonna be moving backwards. Charge onto the rail in the normal manner and lock up in the 50/50 position. Near the middle or end of the rail, push your trailing foot behind you, turning your shoulders and hips so that your butt is facing down the hill. Stay centered and over your board and the rail, leaning slightly downhill. Get your leading hand way out over your heelside edge. Turn your head to keep your eyes on the end of the rail and on the landing. At the end of the rail snap your trailing foot back underneath you using your hips. Stomp down the landing and ride it out. Bang! Do it again!

When you are really comfortable with the ride-on rails, it's time to take these moves to the *ollie-on* rails (rails that require mini jumps or ollies to get on).

Tip: On your first few attempts at the flash to frontside boardslide, you don't need to get your board perpendicular to the rail. Start by flashing it out just a little bit, and as you get more comfortable really push that back foot out and get your board super-sideways.

OLLIE-ON FLAT BOX, 50/50 SLIDE

Ollie-on flat box, 50/50 slide. Here fifteen-year-old Nichole Mason is handling the box perfectly, popping on with an easy ollie, staying centered and low throughout the slide, and driving off through the run-out.

When you are comfortable with the ride-on features it's time to progress to *ollie-on* or *air-on* features. This means it's gonna take a little air to get onto the feature. Power onto the box in your athletic stance with a little ollie, being sure to lift your tip up over the front of the feature. Look to the end of the box, stay centered and forward on your board and drive toward the landing. You can even point with your leading hand to the landing. When you come to the end of the slide, power off the box, stomping your board down on the landing. Continue pointing your board down the hill and ride out the landing.

OLLIE-ON FLAT RAIL, BOARDSLIDE

Pop off the takeoff with a powerful ollie, making sure to get high enough to clear the start of the rail. Keep your arms up away from your body and your head up, looking to the end of the rail. Turn your board perpendicular by twisting your feet, hips, and shoulders 90 degrees and bang onto the rail. Keep your knees bent, and stay nice and low. It's important to lean forward (downhill) when you are locked into the slide. (A good rule is to

Ollie-on flat rail, boardslide.

keep your elbows over your knees and your head out over your toe-side edge.) At the end of the rail snap back into downhill position, stomp it down, and ride it out.

Tip: Take a bit more speed into this trick.

NEXT STEPS ON RAILS

If you go to a few resorts you'll probably see every one of these species of rails. Take cues from these riders to shape your own rail-riding style.

Style on the the kink. (Rider: Rachel Nelson)

Down Rail

Boardslide.

Frontside boardslide. (Rider: Leslie Glen)

Frontside tail press. (Rider: Rachel Nelson)

C-Rail

Frontside boardslide.

Boardslide. (Rider: Tori Koski)

Box

Boardslide. (Rider: Leslie Glen)

Frontside rail press. (Rider: Rachel Nelson)

50/50 slide. (Rider: Jonathan Blank)

Frontside boardslide. (Rider: Matt Ladley)

Kink

Boardslide.

50/50 slide. (Rider: Jonathan Blank)

50/50 slide. (Rider: Rachel Nelson)

Rainbow

Frontside boardslide. (Rider: Ali Kavari)

50/50 slide. (Rider: Brent Hermanusen)

Nose press. (Rider: Ricky Rodriguez)

Flat Rail

Frontside boardslide. (Rider: Rachel Nelson)

Boardslide. (Rider: Josh Moses)

Frontside tail press. (Rider: Robert Blank)

Up-Flat-Down Rail

50/50 slide.

50/50 slide. (Rider: Clair Bidez)

50/50 slide. (Rider: Matt Peterson)

Frontside boardslide. (Rider: Alex Gobel)

Goalpost 50/50 slide. (Rider: Andrew "Droid" Steward)

CHAPTER 5

Wood

Your board allows you to shred surfaces with smoothness that's impossible in other board sports or skiing. With your board you can be busting through the woods when suddenly a disfigured, twisted stump pops up in your path, and without thinking you can just ollie right onto it—crack!—ride right over it, and head on down though the woods.

This chapter will walk you through the basics of riding lumber. Wood awareness on the snowboarding hill will open up a whole different realm of snowboarding fun. Wood is for shredding. It's something surfers can't ride; rarely do skaters slide wood; and when skiers ride logs it just doesn't really work. So check out this chapter, and check out the sidebar by my friend Bob Aubrey—truly a log jibber extraordinaire. Then get into the woods and find yourself a small log and some stumps to jib. Soon you will know the gratification of schralping wood.

50/50 SLIDE ON A FLAT LOG

About 10 feet above your log of choice, stop to set up and check out the approach. In some cases you may need to step out of your bindings and use your board to groom the run-in to ensure a smooth transition onto the log. (Smoothing the approach is an especially good idea on your first few attempts.) Once you've scoped and groomed the approach, drop in on it, pointing your board directly at the log. Take no turns; stay completely

50/50 slide on a flat log.

A Sylvan Meditation

Wood. As snowboarders we're constantly drawn to it. Every aspen rainbow, stump, log slide, and piece of wood somehow beckons us to ride it. Maybe it's because at the core of every board is a fallen tree trying to reunite with its brethren in the forest and warn them of their potential fate. Or maybe it's just because sliding wood is one of the most fun and unique aspects of our sport.

Unlike rails and other features you might find in your local snowboard park, most log slides are found deep in the woods surrounded by other trees—trees that won't think twice about dealing you a bad hand if you don't fully commit, and jump off too early. Combine that with the facts that most logs

(Rider: Bob Aubrey)

actually move to the left or right by a foot while being ridden, and that you constantly have to adjust for knots and bumps, and you've got a recipe for either pure adrenaline or bloody Chiclets.

They say that variety is the spice of life, and the same holds true for log slides. Every log is different. There's no manufacturing facility or standard for building them. They're usually created by the diehard locals who invade the mountain every summer with ropes, saws, power drills, and a creative vision to build something new.

With no judges to impress, no media circus, and no money on the line, a lot of pros won't step to some of the logs that are lurking out there. But on the other hand, the rush of actually stomping a boardslide on one of those giant dinosaur-sized aspen rainbows will leave you with a stoke like no other.

—Bob Aubrey
Freelance writer and log kingpin

committed in your straight-line approach. You want to be nice and low in your athletic stance. Get your arms up away from your body for balance. You can lean back a little on your board in preparation for the stickiness of the log.

Power onto the log by pulling your tip up off the snow with a wheelie-like motion. Stay low and solid, centered in your stance and locked onto the log during the 50/50 slide, looking to the end of the log. At the end of the slide, bend your knees in preparation for the landing. Power off the log, driving toward the run-out. Stomp the landing while continuing to look forward through the run-out.

RIDE THE RAINBOW

Now that you are cleaning flat logs, you gotta go search out some rainbow logs. A rainbow is simply a tree that's top has been bent over and buried by snow; its trunk is arched like a rainbow. Rainbows come in all shapes and sizes. Some occur naturally, others have been shaped by hand. Some are ridged or bumpy, and others are nice, smooth, C-shaped curves, but they all offer challenges and rewards. Attack the rainbow!

Get set up 10 or 15 feet above the rainbow. Keep your eyes focused at the beginning of the log and point your board straight at it. Power onto the log with a small ollie. Now get your eyes up and look to the end of the rainbow. Stay low and centered over your board and square on the log. Drive down the rainbow and slide off onto the snow and through the run-out. Stop, hike it, do it again, then find, or build, a bigger rainbow. Find the pot of gold!

Riding the rainbow. (Rider: Josh Moses)

THE STUMP OLLIE

Stumps are so fun! At any resort or ski area you can find all shapes and sizes of stumps. As a progressive snowboarder out to have the most fun possible, you *must* ollie, jib, and bonk the stump. It's good to ollie completely over the stump, but I like to give the wood a good knock on the way over.

Find a small stump to start on. Approach the stump slowly and stay low in your solid athletic stance. About 8 or 10 feet before the stump, get set by bending your knees and waist, getting *super*-low. Just before the stump, start to come out of your low position with a wheelie motion, getting the tip of your board way up and flexing your board back on its tail. Use the power of the board's flex to pop your ollie, really

Stump ollie.

getting your knees way up to your chest. Let your board bump up and over the stump and absorb the shock with your knees. Stay centered and forward over your board on the top of the stump. Keep your tip up as you come off the stump by shifting your weight to your rear foot. Keep your eyes focused toward the landing. Stomp it down and ride it out.

PICNIC TABLE SLIDE

Picnic table slide.

The picnic table combines an ollie and a slide. You will find a designated table for jibbing in most terrain parks. Use it, and don't wreck any other tables.

Approach the table in your super-low ollie stance. Pop your ollie about 2 feet before the start of the table, getting the tip of your board up over the edge. Slide the table, staying powerful and aggressive in your stance. Keep your eyes forward and stay centered, low, and forward over your board. Keep your tip up as you come off the table. Stomp down the landing on the snow and ride it out.

NEXT STEPS ON WOOD

As you progress on wood and your confidence improves, the features you ride will get bigger. Check out the wood these riders have found, and the styles they use to ride it.

50/50 up-flat-down log.

Build Your Own Log Jib

If there aren't any logs to ride at your local hill, you'll have to build one. The easiest log jib you can build is the flat log. Find a good dead log in the woods. Set the downhill end on a stump and bury about 2 feet of the uphill end in the snow so it doesn't move. Or set the log in the other direction, to make it an ollie-on jib. I have used saws, hatchets, hammers, and really big nails to attach logs to stumps.

Get creative with the construction of your jibs. You can build one with logs going up a stump and then down the other side. Or lean a log onto a low branch; ride up it and off one side.

To build a rainbow you must get on the hill before the snow gets deep. Bend a tree down and tie the end of it off to another tree, a downed log, or a large stake in the ground. When the snow gets deep it will bury the tied-down end. Then you will have a killer rainbow to ride. Try to build an entire secret log line at your local mountain. Then you will be a logger.

One important request: When you are building wood to ride, don't kill any trees. Slide the ones that are already dead. Trees are good.

Flat Log

50/50 stall on fat flat log. (Rider Jake Black)

Flash to boardslide on a Breck flat log.

50/50 on a goalpost flat log. (Rider: Mike Markowitz)

Rainbow Log

Frontside boardslide on a Breck rainbow.

50/50 over a powder-covered bow. (Rider: Jim Duffy)

50/50 on a snowy day in Vail. (Rider: Ryan Neff)

Jibbing the mini bow. (Rider: Nick Larson)

Stump

Spring stump bonk.

Stump ollie. (Rider: Andrew "Droid" Steward)

Twisted wood ollie.

Tail bonk. (Rider: Andrew "Droid" Steward)

Picnic Table

Table ollie.

Tail press table ride. (Rider: Andrew "Droid" Steward)

Flash to boardslide on a table.

Double table slide at a Copper jib contest. (Rider: Rachel Nelson)

Frontside air. (Rider: Dylan Bidez)

CHAPTER 6

Halfpipe

The halfpipe has evolved from a barely visible blip on the ski resort map into a giant, groomed, and perfected feature. Just a few years ago riders were digging walls by hand to emulate a skateboard halfpipe. Now resorts are spending big money on technologically advanced halfpipe shapers to cater to the progressive rider.

The halfpipe is everything it's cracked up to be. It's an incredible rush. For me, the real attraction is that you get several hits that send you skyward into airs and tricks in a short amount of space and time. In between these airs and tricks you must have the technical skills to hang onto your edge and position your body to keep your ride flowing. The aestheticism and the feeling a solid pipe ride can give you is unmatched by any sport or art form I have experienced.

That said, the pipe is probably the most difficult discipline in this book. A high-quality pipe can be a huge, daunting set of transitioned icy snow walls, full of good riders snapping airs, spins, and flips well out of the pipe's lip. Don't be intimidated! Approach the pipe in a calm and systematic way. The pipe will take some time to learn. Be patient, take it slow, and master one skill at a time. Follow the progression I have laid out in this chapter, use visualization, and practice the drills at the end of the chapter. Don't sweat other riders in the pipe; just be aware of what is going on around you and the other riders will usually give you all the space you need. Do these things and you will be killing the pipe and loving it. And check Bud Keene's sidebar for more insight and for a history of the halfpipe.

PIPE LAYOUT

At the top of the pipe is the *drop-in deck*, where you get in the lineup and wait to drop into the pipe. The pipe has a *flat bottom* (which is what it sounds like) and a *left wall* and a *right wall* (as seen looking downhill from the drop-in deck). The right wall for a regular-

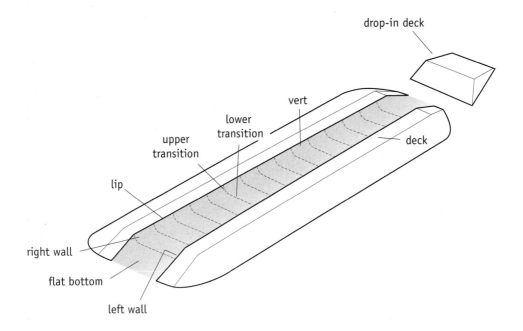

Layout of a halfpipe.

footer is the frontside, or toe-side wall, and the left wall is the backside or heel-side wall. For a goofy-footer the right wall is the backside and the left wall is the frontside. Both walls have a *lower transition* (where the flat begins to curve upward), an *upper transition* (where the curve meets the vertical section), a *vert* (the vertical section), a *lip* (the upper edge), and a *deck* (the flat horizontal surface beyond the lip).

Pipes come in small, medium, and large. The large size, known as the *super pipe*, is maintained and shaped with a machine called the Zaugg Pipe Monster, which cuts a perfect 18- to 22-foot-high pipe wall with an elliptical curve from bottom to lip. Medium-sized pipes have walls 10 to 15 feet high, and small pipes are 5 to 8 feet high. Don't be fooled by the sizes: A smaller pipe is not necessarily easier to ride. In a sense, the super pipe can be the easiest pipe to learn how to ride, if you can master the intimidation of its sheer size. Its long transitions, or *trannies*, give you more time to think about what you are doing, and things don't happen as quickly as in a pipe with a shorter transition. However, I recommend that you learn on a medium-sized pipe if you have the option. This will remove the pressure of having a lot of really good riders around as you learn. When you are comfortable in the regular-sized pipe, move on to the super pipe. The mini pipe is fun and especially good for young kids to get the feel for transition, but the real ride is in the bigger pipes.

Halfpipe Genesis

In the beginning there was the wave. When surfers first steered 100-pound planks of wood into the path of a wave, and then stood up, it was the action-sports equivalent of the first prehistoric species waddling ashore from the primordial ooze, never to return. A new pastime had been born, a new art form—some might argue, a new *life* form. This was the birth of man's love affair with *transition*.

Then came the skateboarders. As films like *Dogtown* document, those California surfers first conceived the skateboard as a dry-land training tool, and they practiced the same movements on flat ground and slight hills that they were performing in the water. But soon, and naturally, they wondered: "Where's the wave?" So they found it—first in the form of culverts and drainage ditches paved over by engineers, then in backyard swimming pools drained off for the winter or for repairs. Later, they picked up

(Rider: Bud Keene)

their tools and made the waves of their dreams, and these ramps and half pipes, made of wood, steel, or concrete, are now ridden with gusto from coast to coast and around the world.

When snowboarding's inventors started experimenting with early prototypes in the late 1970s, they were surfers looking to bring their skills, and their way of looking at the world, to snow-covered mountains. At first they were like the early SoCal surfers-turned-skaters, turning on and slashing the snow much like its liquid cousin. Then some skaters got into it—skaters who by this time had been raised on transition. Once again the question was asked: "Where is the wave?" So now with their snowboards, they again found it. First in places like Donner Ski Ranch and Tahoe City, where nature's transitions were enhanced with shovels and hard work, and later at winter resorts worldwide. The art of riding transition had been brought full circle, only now the wave was frozen.

Today's halfpipes are perfect, North Shore–size waves (20-plus feet), and they're safer and more fun than ever. If you're fortunate to live near a resort with a well-maintained pipe, use it. It's a ton of fun. Just make sure to pay respect to the history that put it there. It might even help your surfing and skating.

—Bud Keene
Head Halfpipe Coach, U.S. Snowboard Team

HALFPIPE ETIQUETTE

Above the pipe there will be loose lines of riders waiting on both sides of the drop-in deck. Get in the lineup on either side, or right in the middle, and stay on your feet. The lineup will drop in more or less on alternating sides. The people on the left will drop toward the right wall for their first hit, and the riders on the right will drop toward the left wall for their first hit.

Lining up at the drop-in deck.

PIPE DRILLS

Practice this stuff out on a groomed run to get more comfortable with your pipe riding.

Large-Radius Turning Drill

On a wide-groomed run make large-radius turns, concentrating on getting across the fall line between turns. Get really low when you are crossing the fall line and starting to make your turn. In the middle of your turn, extend up out of the turn with a front-to-back motion and pop onto your next edge. Get really low again (overexaggerate your low athletic stance) when crossing the fall line.

Crossing the fall line simulates crossing the pipe's flat bottom, and popping from edge to edge simulates your air and transfer to your new edge. The super-overexaggerated flexion and extension simulates your pumping motion (see "Pumping" sidebar on page 100) on the pipe's transitions.

Rail-Grab Drill

This drill was shown to me by snowboarding legend Dave Dowd.

As with the large-radius turning drill, make big wide turns, getting across the fall line and popping from edge to edge. When you cross the fall line, get super-low by bending at the knees and waist. When you are on a heel-side turn, grab your toe-side edge between your feet with your trailing hand. When you are on your toe-side turn, grab your heel-side edge between your feet with your leading hand. It ain't easy, especially on a toe-side turn.

This drill will help you become super-comfortable when you're way low. It will also teach you where your edges are for second-nature grabs. It's an awesome all-around drill. Give it a go!

When you get to the front of the line call, "Dropping!" with your hand up, and make eye contact with the other riders who are at the front of the lines. You can even ask these riders to give you some space before they drop in. (It's easy. Just ask. Almost everyone is cool with that.) And remember the Golden Rule about doing unto others: *Never* pass another rider during their pipe ride.

HALFPIPE PROGRESSION

Falling leaf drill. (*A note on the photograph:* To prevent placing some images on top of one another, it was necessary to exaggerate the distance between some steps. The steps that are connected by a dotted line should be performed at roughly the same location.)

Falling Leaf

To start your halfpipe progression and get the feel for the transition of the walls, do the falling leaf drill a few times. In this drill you will float and flow down the pipe like a leaf or a feather on the air, always remaining on the same edge.

Sideslip into the pipe on your heelside edge. Traverse to your backside wall, staying on your heel edge. Stay low in your athletic stance and go nice and slow. As you reach the transition, ride up it 3 or 4 feet with a *pumping* motion (see "Pumping" sidebar), extending your legs up out of your low stance as you climb the wall. Keep your shoulders parallel to your board and the angle of the wall's transition as you climb. At the peak of your momentum, pump back down the wall by bending your knees and getting back into your

Pumping

Pumping the transitions of the pipe walls is crucial to the flow of your pipe ride. The concept is simple: as you climb the wall, you will extend your legs to propel your upper body out of its low position; then, as you come back down the wall, you will bend/flex your legs to get back into your low stance.

Your first pipe attempts will take place on the lower part of the pipe's transitions. Here, your pumping motion will be quick: pop up out of your low stance and quickly return to your stance on the way down.

As you graduate to higher heights, the pump will be a more gradual, fluid motion: extend up the wall smoothly, and retract slowly as you return downward.

The speed of your pumping motion will also be dictated by the size of the pipe you are riding. In a mini pipe, your pumping motions will be quick and decisive. As you graduate to a super pipe, you will need to be patient with your pump.

Pumping is a "feel" skill. Check out the demonstrations in this chapter, observe other riders, then get in there and feel it out for yourself.

It will click.

low athletic stance. You will be going fakie as you head down and across the pipe toward the next wall, still on your heelside edge. Look where you are going. Keep your head and eyes up. When you reach the next wall, again pump up the transition by extending your legs out of your low athletic stance. At the peak of your momentum, pump back down the wall, riding regular to the next wall. Repeat this all the way down the pipe, and do it for a few runs until you are comfortable with the flow.

You can practice the falling leaf on a groomed run to get ready for the halfpipe drill.

Drop-In

Frontside Wall

Now that you have the falling leaf down, it's time to learn the drop-in. In your low stance, come down the drop-in, stay to the far left (if you ride regular), and head straight toward the deck. Don't ride all the

Drop-in to your frontside wall.

way to the top of the deck. Instead, ride about halfway up the deck's "on ramp"—this will be a less intimidating starting point. From there, turn toward the lip, with your board pointed down and across the pipe at about a 30-degree angle to the fall line. As you reach the lip, power your weight over your front foot to tip yourself downward onto the wall. Flatten your base as you ride down the transition. Engage your toe edge as you reach the flat bottom, and flow toward the opposite wall. Keep your head up, looking toward the wall. No sweat; it's easy.

Backside Wall

Drop-in to your backside wall.

Now let's try dropping in from the other side. In your low athletic stance come down the drop-in deck, stay to the far right (if you ride regular), and ride partway up the "on ramp" of the pipe's deck. Turn toward the lip, with your board pointed down and across the pipe. As you reach the lip, stay low and power over your front foot. Ride down the trannie on your flat base, then engage your heel edge and flow to your first hit.

Tip: To become a good pipe rider, you need to be able to drop in from both sides.

Ride the wall—frontside.

Ride the Wall

Frontside

To start this progression, drop in and slowly head for your frontside wall. Approach the frontside wall nice and low and ride it just like you are riding a banked wall on the side of a run.

As you start to climb the wall, begin to extend, or *pump*. Wait for the peak of your momentum, then switch your edges and pump back down the wall, bending your knees and crouching into your athletic stance.

Backside

In your balanced athletic stance approach your backside wall on your heels with your head up and your leading hand over your heel-side edge. On the low part of the transition

Ride the wall—backside.

start to pump up the wall, coming up out of your athletic stance. At the peak of your momentum turn your leading shoulder down toward the flat bottom, switch your edge to your toe-side, and pump back down the transition and return to your athletic stance. Head for the next wall, this time trying to get a little higher up the trannie.

Get into riding the walls. Really bend your knees and your waist, going up and down with a flowing, grooving motion.

Tip: Commit your weight into the pipe by getting your head over your toe-side edge.

Hop Turn

Frontside

After practicing and getting a really good feel for riding the wall, start to make a hop turn at the peak of your momentum. Stay low, pump your legs as you climb the wall such that you'll hop six inches to a foot off the wall when you reach the peak of your momentum.

Hop turn—frontside.

Turn 180 degrees by turning your head, shoulders, and hips back toward the pipe. Land on your heelside edge and pump back down the wall and return to your athletic stance.

Practice this a bunch of times, and when you feel more comfortable, start to carry a little more speed and do the hop turn higher on the transition.

Backside

Now head for the backside wall. Pump up the wall, hop off it, and turn 180 degrees back down into the pipe by turning your head, hips, and shoulders. Stomp your air down, then

Hop turn—backside.

quickly transfer to your toe-side edge, staying nice and centered front-to-back on the board. Pump back down the wall.

Let the Wall Send You

In this step in the progression, you'll start to let the halfpipe wall do the work of popping you into the air. You'll be carrying more speed from the trannie into the vert.

Frontside

Come at the pipe wall faster than before, staying low in your athletic stance. Keep your shoulders parallel with the wall's transition as you climb higher. Stay centered over your board. Wait until your board reaches the vert, then do a subtle ollie, bringing your knees up to your chest. The vert and the momentum you are carrying will send you fluidly into the air. Don't force it and try to go big; your first airs should only be six inches or a foot high. Turn your head, shoulders, hips, and leading hand back into the pipe. Stay centered

Let the wall send you—frontside.

and set it down, pumping down the wall back to the old comfortable athletic stance. So fun.

Tip: To gain speed, angle your board more toward the fall line. To slow down, point your board more toward the opposite wall.

Backside

Approach the wall with some speed, driving and pumping and leading yourself up the wall with your leading hand. As you reach the vert, extend your legs subtly and ollie gently off the wall, but let the vert do most of the work. Only try for six inches or a foot of air. Keep your head and shoulders over your toe-side edge.

Tip: As you get higher, you must commit your weight into the pipe. You do this by matching the angle of your shoulders with the angle of the wall's transition and vert. When you reach the vert, really drop your head and shoulders out over your toe-side edge.

Let the wall send you—backside.

Air above the Lip

Frontside

This is the fourth and final step to conquering the frontside pipe wall. Angle your board closer to the fall line for even more speed. Your eyes need to be up, looking past the lip. Get stoked! Stay low, and be aggressive.

Ride up the wall in your athletic stance, staying low longer—wait for the lip. Keeping your leading hand over your heel-side edge and turn your upper body to face, or *address*, the wall—as you would the fall line in a turn. As the tip of your board reaches the lip, flatten your base and extend your legs with a subtle ollie skyward, up and out of the lip. Pop off your tail. Bring your knees up to your chest in the air and grab frontside. Turn your head, shoulders, hips, and leading hand back into the pipe. Lead yourself with your leading hand and look at the wall for your landing. Extend your legs subtly for landing;

Air out of the lip—frontside.

stomp it down flat onto your base, staying centered; and pump down the wall on your heel-side edge while settling into your athletic stance. Charge at the next wall.

Tip: Don't ollie *in* toward the flat bottom; ollie *up* and *out*: Drive toward the sky. Keep in mind that the pipe wall will do most of the work to get you into the air. The ollie is a subtlety, especially when you are just beginning to venture outside the lip.

Backside

Stay on your heel-side edge through the flat bottom and up the transition. In your low athletic stance, power up the wall with your head up, looking past the lip and toward the sky. Address the wall with your leading hand over your heel-side edge, staying open to the wall. As you reach the vert, begin to extend your legs out of your low stance and flatten

Method air out of the lip.

your base. Pop a subtle ollie off your tail, powering up and out of the lip. Bring your knees up in the air and grab method (leading hand to heel-side edge between your feet or just in front of your leading foot). Turn your shoulders and hips back into the pipe and look to your landing on the wall. Extend your legs and stomp your air down onto your flat base. Ride down the wall back into your stance and pick up your toe-side edge, charging to your frontside wall. Killer.

EDGE TRANSFER

A common mistake that occurs when you are carrying more speed and getting more air in the pipe is landing on your downhill edge. Remember, when you are airing off your toe-side edge, you will land with your base flat and then *transfer* to your heel-side edge. When you air off your heel-side edge, you land flat on your base and then transfer to your toe-side edge. Toes to heels, and heels to toes. This principle is referred to as *edge transfer*.

NEXT STEPS IN THE HALFPIPE

Frontside Grabs

Check out these different pipe tricks and grabs and the riders' individual styles.

Frontside Air

(Rider: Dylan Bidez)

(Rider: Shawn White)

(Rider: Chauncy Sorenson)

Lien Air

(Rider: Zach Meisner)

(Rider: Todd Richards)

(Rider: Dylan Bidez)

Stale Fish

(Rider: Dylan Bidez)

(Rider: Clair Bidez)

Mute Air

(Rider: Zack Black)

(Rider: Zeke Hersh)

(Rider: Jarrett Packer)

Tail Grab

(Rider: Zack Black)

(Rider: Clair Bidez)

(Rider: Dylan Bidez)

Backside Grabs
Method Air

(Rider: J.J. Thomas)

(Rider: Ryan Knapton)

(Rider: Clair Bidez)

Tail Grab

(Rider: Ryan Knapton)

(Rider: Jarrett Packer)

Mute Air

(Rider: Dylan Bidez)

(Rider: Leslie Glen)

(Rider: Jarrett Packer)

Indy Air

(Rider: Travis Rice)

(Rider: Todd Richards)

Fresh Fish

(Rider: Dylan Bidez)

(Rider: John Schurke)

A Grab Bag

Frontside tip grab.

Melon to fakie. (Rider: J.J. Thomas)

Crooked cop.

Crail.

Japan air.

Backside tip grab. (Rider: Todd Richards)

(Rider: Jake Black)

CHAPTER 7

More Tricks of the Trade

Sometimes you are presented with the challenge of making it across a flat snow-cat track or a random flat spot on the hill. Here are two techniques to help you deal with the flats, followed by a few more fun tricks.

THE MOMENTUM LEAP

Momentum leap.

The *momentum leap* will get you a little glide across a small flat spot like you might find at the top or bottom of a chairlift. Get set with your board perpendicular to the direction you want to go. Crouch down really low with your arms behind you, then spring forward while throwing your arms out in front of you. While you're in the air, turn your board 90 degrees such that you land with your board pointed in your direction of travel. Use the momentum you have created with the forward leap to glide to the pitch. Pump your arms and upper body to help feed the momentum.

Tip: The momentum leap is also effective if you need to generate a bit more speed at the drop into a park feature like a kicker or a rail, or even the halfpipe.

THE ARMY MAN WALK

Army man walk.

The *army man walk* (also known as the *penguin walk*) will get you across flats or into position to drop into a halfpipe or a park kicker. Get your board perpendicular to the direction of travel and, starting with small movements, begin a waddling movement with your feet. Use your shoulders and arms to get rhythm going—pop from tail to tip to tail to tip, while leaning forward and using the board's flex to build momentum. To help visualize it, think about how a kid would make a plastic toy soldier walk. Not only is this an effective way to move on flats, but it's fun. It also looks really funny, so you can crack your friends up.

BUTTERING

Tail butter. (Rider: Jake Black)

Buttering is simply balancing over the nose or tail of your board while sliding along down a groomed run.

Tail Butter

Tail butter. (Rider: Jason Troth)

To learn the *tail butter*, find a nice mellow pitch on a groomed run. Start really slow and small; get all your weight back on the tail of your board to get some wheelie-like motions going. Pull up on your front leg to flex the middle of your board up and lift its nose off the snow. When you are comfortable popping a wheelie along the snow for short distances in a tail butter, try the nose butter.

Nose Buttter

To start the *nose butter*, slide sideways and begin moving all your weight over your front leg and the nose of your board (1). Flex your board in the middle by pulling up with

Nose butter.

your trailing leg, lifting the tail off the snow with a fluid motion (2). Don't jerk your tail off the snow. Start small, lifting the tail only a few inches. After you become comfortable balancing over the nose of your board, try to pop into the nose butter with an ollie and hold the position, buttering along for long distances (3-6). When you start to lose your balance, use the snap in the board's flex to pop your weight back over the board and cruise on down the run.

As you get better balancing over the tip of your board, mix up different combinations of butters. Try a tail butter to a nose butter or a nose butter to fakie. Check it out—it's super fun and will make you and your friends laugh.

LAYBACK SLIDE

Layback slide. (Rider: Rachel Nelson)

(Rider: Jake Black)

The *layback slide* is a move unique to board sports. Surfers mastered the layback, then skaters took it to the pavement, and then snowboarders adapted it to the snow. There is nothing like a good layback.

The layback is a frontside slash executed on a snowbank of any kind. Approach a snowbank with a good bit of speed. As your board reaches the top of the bank, snap a hard heelside slash, throwing your board sideways. You must stay low, with your legs bent all the while. At the same moment throw your trailing hand back behind you and drag it in the snow. Try to really snap the snow with your heel-side edge and get it to fly in the air. Push yourself back up over your board with your trailing hand and ride it out low over your stick, looking back at your slash and snow cloud. The layback is super-fun in soft snow whether it's slush or powder. Snap!

(Rider: Rob Bak)

CHAPTER 8

Cross-Training

If you want to be the best snowboarder you can be, you have to stay active and keep your body strong. This chapter offers some good stuff to do in the off-season to keep your Jedi rider skills flowing.

SKATEBOARDING

If you don't know how to skate, start out by just pushing around in a smooth parking lot or rolling around the edges of your local skate park. Once you feel good about pumping your skateboard and rolling around, step to the ramp. You can learn to pump on any shape or size of ramp. A big ramp is generally better because the radius of the transition is longer and more gradual and you have time to think about what you're doing. Watch other people who are out there skating and imitate their motions. Wear a helmet and pads.

Pumping the Halfpipe

Get in the middle of the pipe and give a mellow push toward the transition. Get your feet in position and stay low in your athletic stance. When you reach the transition, drive up

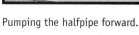
Pumping the halfpipe forward.

it with a pumping motion, extending up out of your low stance. Call on your snowboarding strength and emulate your motions from the snowboarding halfpipe. The motions are very similar. At the peak of your momentum turn your head back toward the transition going backwards and pump back down the transition, getting back into your low athletic stance. Look to the next transition, and as you reach it, drive up it again with a pumping motion. As you feel more and more comfortable on the bottom part of the transition, pump harder and go faster, and drive to the coping (the lip) of the ramp. Once you are comfortable getting up nice and high on that transition, you can progress to the kick turn.

Pumping the halfpipe fakie.

Tip: Keep your shoulders parallel to the transition. Keep in mind the motion of pumping in the snow halfpipe—the motions are the same.

Backside Kick Turn

Backside kick turn.

To work on the *kick turn*, approach the ramp's transition going slow and staying in your stance. Pump up the transition, and when you reach the peak of your momentum, pressure your tail slightly, picking up your front wheels. Turn your hips, shoulders, and head, and snap your body through a 180-degree turn. You will be turning your back to the top of the ramp for the backside kick turn. Completing the 180, punch down over your front wheels with your front foot and pump back down the ramp. Get in your stance while driving across the flat bottom of the ramp and repeat the pump up the transition to the kick turn. When you are comfortable kick-turning on the lower transition, pick up some speed by pumping harder and do your kick turn higher on the wall.

Tip: A good way to begin to feel the motion of the kick turn is to mess around doing 180s on flat pavement.

Frontside Kick Turn

Frontside kick turn.

Try a few frontside 180s on the flat pavement, then take it to the ramp. Start low on the trannie and pump up that wall. Prepare for the frontside kick turn by opening up in your stance and turning your shoulders to face the transition. At the peak of your momentum, kick the tail slightly; turn your head, shoulders, and hips; and snap your feet 180 degrees. Drive down with your front foot over your front wheels and pump back down the wall. Repeat. Try not to get dizzy. Once you've got that, it's time to grind!

Dropping In

Start on a small ramp to learn the *drop-in*. Stand on the deck of the ramp and place the tail of your board over the coping with your trailing foot. Get your front foot in position on the tip of your board and stomp down, pounding your front wheels down on the trannie. *Lean forward* and power down the transition of the ramp over your front foot.

Tip: The drop-in is intimidating at first. Be confident and don't hesitate. As long as you lean forward, you will get it. If you are having a hard time with the commitment, have a friend literally hold your hands as you drop.

Downhill Skateboarding

The downhill skate is super-fun and is a fantastic simulation of cruising on a snowboard. Start out just cruising around a smooth parking lot or tennis court. When you are comfortable pushing the board and gliding around on the flats, take it to a mellow hill. Really call on your snowboarding skills to ride your downhill board. As you get more and more comfortable, take your ride to bigger and bigger hills such as bike paths or big office

Downhill skateboarding.

parking lots, or parking structures. Crashing on a downhill board is rough (consider it *not an option*), so move onto higher speeds cautiously and wear your pads. Practice *running out* a ride (jumping off the board and running it out) as well as the *foot drag* (taking your trailing foot off the board and dragging the bottom of your shoe to slow down).

CORE-STRENGTHENING EXERCISES

To be capable of riding hard and well and learning new skills, it's important to have a strong *core*—the middle of your body, including your abdomen, lower back, and hips. Here are a few simple exercises you can do to stay strong. Mix two or three of these exercises up every time you do them so your body doesn't get used to a pattern. (I recommend stretching before you do these exercises and stretches. Warming up can be as easy as taking a short walk or a run, or doing a bit of skateboarding.) If, during the exercises that follow, your core muscles get sore, you are doing them right. Get strong for snowboarding!

Balance Ball Crunch

Start in a reclined position and roll your chin toward your belly button, flexing your abdomen. Start with three sets of fifteen, then add more as you feel comfortable. I recommend you add another rep to this routine every day.

Balance Ball Leg Roll/Reverse Leg Roll

Balance ball leg roll.

Reverse ball leg roll.

Start in the push-up position and roll the ball to you by flexing your knees. In addition to strengthening your core, this one is also good for your quadriceps, hamstrings, and the tops of your hips. Do three sets of five and add more to stay sore.

Balance Ball Shuffle

Uh, this one kinda hurts. Start in the push-up position with your feet spread apart on the ball. Shuffle the ball from side to side until your toes bump the ground on either side. Do three sets of five and move up from there.

Balance Ball Superman

Lay with your lower middle balanced on the ball. Raise your opposite leg and arm and hold it nice and flat for a twenty count. Do five sets.

Balance Ball Push-up

This one is just like a regular push-up except your feet are balanced on the ball. This move is a great way to keep your back, shoulders, chest, arms, and wrists strong. You can try a few pushing up on your fingertips to strengthen your hands and wrists.

Medicine Ball Lunge

This exercise is a great one for your core and your quads. From a standing position step forward, dropping your knee to the ground while lowering the medicine ball to your side. Do three sets of ten. You can also do it moving backwards (reverse lunge). If your quads get sore, you are doing it right. I also recommend squats to strengthen your legs.

The Gyro Ball

The most common injuries in snow-boarding are to the wrists, and the gyro exerciser is a fantastic tool to strengthen your wrists, fingers, and forearms. This is basically a ball within a ball: You get it rotating with a circular motion in your wrist, and in about two seconds it starts to burn the muscles in your forearms, fingers, and wrists.

STRETCHING

Stretching should be a daily part of your life as a snowboarder. Unfortunately, it is often neglected, and that neglect increases your chances of injury. Stay limber; stretch.

Leg Raise for Hamstrings

Lie on your back and raise your leg, holding your calf. To feel this stretch in your calf as well as your hamstring, point your toe to your chin.

Straddle

Open your legs until you feel the stretch in your groin. Drop your head and let the weight of your head stretch out your back. This gives a good stretch in your legs and back.

"Figure 4" for Hips

Lie on your back, cross one leg over the other, and grab the knee of your bottom leg. You will feel this stretch in the outside of your hip on your crossed leg. Lie back during this stretch, relaxing your back and neck.

Butterfly

In a seated position, put the soles of your feet together and butterfly your legs. Pull your heels in toward you until you feel the stretch in your groin. I like to get a two-for-one stretch out of this one by dropping my head and stretching out my back.

Hip Push-out

In a standing position, step out with one leg, keeping your feet flat on the ground. Push your front hip out.

Wrists and Fingers

Push your hand down toward your wrist, feeling the stretch in the top of your wrist. Hold the stretch for a twenty count. Bend your hand backwards, feeling the stretch in the underside of your wrist and your fingers. Hold for a twenty count.

The Seal (Core Stretch)

To stretch the front muscles of your abdomen, lie flat on your front then push up with your arms, arching your back and looking to the sky. Bark like a seal.

Numbers in **bold** refer to pages with photos or illustrations

address, 27, 108
age, snowboarding and, 1
air above the lip, 107–**9**
air-on features, 66. *See also* ollie
    entries
apex, 26
army man walk, **132**
Aubrey, Bob, 81, **82**

back seat, **31**
backside grabs, **120–25, 129**
backside hip, **57, 58, 59**
backside wall
    air above the lip, 108–**9**
    dropping in, **101**
    hop turn, 104–6, **105**
    location of, **96**
    riding, 102–**3**
Bak, Rob, **138**
balance ball exercises
    crunch, **145**
    leg rolls, **145**–46
    push-up, **147**
    shuffle, **146**
    Superman, **146**
balanced athletic stance, 17,
    19–20
Berthoud Pass, Colorado, xi
Bidez, Clair, **22, 78, 115, 119, 121**
Bidez, Dylan, 4, **24, 94, 110, 113,**
    115, 119, 124, 127
bindings
    adjustments, 12–14, **13**
    importance of setup, 17
    setup examples, **22–25**
    setup guidelines, 20–**21**
Black, Jake, **2, 25, 46, 49, 51, 53,**
    86, 130, 133, 137
Black, Zack, **116, 118**

Blank, Jonathan, **73, 74**
Blank, Robert, **77**
boardslide position, 63–**64, 68,**
    71, 72, 74, 77
booters, 39. *See also* kickers
boots, **14**–15
Borchardt, Robert, **51**
bottom, flat, 95, **96**
boxes, 61, **66, 72–73**
Burton Performer snowboard, xi
butterfly, **149**
buttering, **133–35**
butt pads, 4–5

camber, **8**
carving a turn, 26
cheese wedges, 39. *See also*
    kickers
completion, 26
core-strengthening exercises,
    144–**48**
core stretch, **150**
crail air, **56, 58, 129**
C-rails, **70–71**
crooked cop, **128**
cross-training, 4, **139–44**

deck, 95, **96**
Decoy board, **11**
directional boards, **11**–12
Dogtown (film), 97
Donner Ski Ranch, 97
double table slide, **93**
Dowd, Dave, 37, 98
downhill skateboarding, **144**
down rails, **68–69**
drop-in deck, 95, **96**
drop-in ramp, **43**
dropping in

backside wall, **101**
frontside wall, **100**–101
halfpipe etiquette, 97–**98**, 99
kicker etiquette, 39–**40**
skateboarding, **143**–44
duck stance, 21

edge transfer, 27, 109
edging, 26
exercises, 4, 144–**48**
extension, **26**, 27

fakie, 20
falling leaf drill, **99**–100
fall line, 20
50/50 position, 62–63
    flash to boardslide, 63–**64, 65**
    on a log, **81**–82, **86, 87, 88–89**
    picnic table slide, **85**
    rail slide, 62–**63**
    slide, **73–76, 78–80**
        up-flat-down log, **85**
figure 4 stretch, **149**
finger stretches, **150**
flash to boardslide
    50/50 position, 63–**64, 65**
    on a log, **87**
    on a table, **93**
flat logs, **81**–82, **86–87**
flat rails, 61
    ollie-on flat rail, boardslide,
    66–67
    ride-on flat rail, 62–**65**
    style examples, **77**
flex (snowboards), 9–11, **10**
flexion, **26**, 27
forward lean, 12–**13**
forward stance, 21
freestyle boards. *See* snowboards

fresh fish, **127**
frontside air, **59**, **110–11**
frontside grabs, **110–19**
frontside hip, **59**
frontside kick turn, **142**–43
frontside position, 64–**65**
    frontside boardslide, **69**, **70**, **73**, **76**, **77**, **79**
    on a rainbow log, **88**
    rail press, **72**
    tail press, **69**, **77**
frontside tip grab, **128**
frontside wall
    air above the lip, 107–**8**
    dropping in, **100**–101
    hop turn, 103–**4**
    location of, **96**
    riding, **102**

gear, 4–5, 7
Glen, Leslie, **69**, **72**, **125**
goalpost 50/50 slide, **80**
Gobel, Alex, **79**
goofy-foot stance, 17–**18**, **21**
grabs. *See also* specific grabs
    examples of, **45**–56
    get the grab, **45**
gyro ball, **148**

halfpipe
    board design for, 8
    drills, 98
    etiquette, 97–**98**, 99
    evolution of, 95, 97
    experience of, 95
    layout of, 95–**96**
    learning, 95, 96
    passing in, 99
    pipe-cutting machines, xii, 96
    progression, **99–109**
    shaping of, 96
    size of, 96
    style examples, **110–29**
hamstring stretch, **148**
The Hard, the Hungry and the Homeless (film), 62
heel cup, **13**
heel ramp, **13**, 14
heel-side large-radius turn, **32**–33

heel-side medium-radius turn, **29**
heel-side rail-grab drill, **37**, 98
heel-side wall, **96**
helmets, 4
Hermanusen, Brent, **76**
Hersh, Zeke, **116**
highback, **13**, 14
hip jumps, **57**–**59**
hip pads, 4–5
hip stretches, **149**
hop turn, 103–6, **104**, **105**

ice packs, 5
indy air, **45**, **48–49**, **126**
initiation, 26
injuries, 4–5, 40, 148

Japan air, **129**
jibs, 11, 85
jumps, 39. *See also* kickers

Kavari, Ali, **76**
Keene, Bud, 95, **97**
Kerney, Harry, **53**
kickers
    advances in, 39
    anatomy of, **43**
    board design for, 8
    dropping in, 39–**40**, **43**
    etiquette, 39–**40**
    experience of, 39
    grabs, **45**–56
    hip jumps, **57–59**
    landing areas, 39, 40, **43**
    learning, 39
    skills, **41**–45
    thoughts while executing, 4
kick turns, **141**–43
kink rails, **67**, **74–75**
Knapton, Ryan, **120**, **122**
knees up in the air, 4
Koski, Tori, **71**

Ladley, Matt, **73**
landing areas, 39, 40, **43**
large-radius turns, 29–**33**, 98
Larson, Nick, **24**
layback slide, **136–37**
left wall, 95, **96**

leg raise, **148**
leg rolls, **145**–46
length of boards, 8
let the wall send you, **106**–7
lien air, **59**, **112–13**
lip, 4, **96**, **107**–9
load the tail, **34**
log slides
    building, 85
    experience of, 82
    style examples, **86–93**
    thoughts while riding, 4
    types of, **81–85**
look past the lip, 4
look to the end, 4
Loveland Pass, Colorado, 62
lower transition, **96**
lumber, riding, 81. *See also* log slides
lunge, medicine ball, **147**

Markowitz, Mike, **23**, **59**, **87**
Mason, Nicholas, **66**
McCafferty, Kyle, **60**
medicine ball lunge, **147**
medium-radius turns, **28**–29
Meisner, Zach, **112**
melon to fakie, **128**
Merriman, Adam, **59**
method air, **54–55**, **59**, **109**, **120–21**
momentum air, **43**–44
momentum leap, **131**–32
Moses, Josh, **77**, **83**
mute air, **52–53**, **116–17**, **124–25**

Nelson, Rachel, **55**, **67**, **69**, **72**, **75**, **77**, **93**, **136**
nose butter, **134–35**
nose press, **76**

offset stance, 20
ollie, 17, **34–35**, **44**
ollie-on features, 66
    boxes, **66**
    rails, 65, **66–67**
    stump, **83–84**
on-snow demos, 7
Otremba, Joe, **54**

Packer, Jarrett, **25**, **117**, **123**, **125**
park kickers, 39. *See also* kickers
penguin walk, **132**
Peterson, Matt, **79**
picnic table slide, **84–85**, **92–93**
pipes. *See* halfpipe
pitch, 62
Premier 157 board, **11**
progression (progressive) snowboarding, 1, 3, 5
property, respect for, 62
pumping motion, 98, 99–100,
139–41

rail-grab drill, **37**, 98
rails. *See also* flat rails
approaches to, 61–**62**
board design for, 8
drills, 64
etiquette, 61
experience of, 61
rules for, 64
thoughts while riding, 4
types of, 61, **67–79**
rainbow logs, 82, **83**, 85, **88–89**
rainbow rails, **76**
regular stance, 17–**18**, **21**
Rice, Travis, **126**
Richards, Todd, **112**, **126**, **129**
ride-on box, 61
ride-on flat rail, 62–**65**
riding the wall, **102**–3
right wall, 95–**96**
Rocky Mountain Snowboard
Series, xii
Rodriguez, Ricky, **76**
roller air, **41–42**
rollover, **42**
rotation, 27

safety, 4–5
Schurke, John, **127**
seal stretch, **150**
short-radius turns, **27–28**
sidecut, 8, **9**
skateboarding, 97
backside kick turn, **141–42**
downhill, **144**

dropping in, **143**–44
frontside kick turn, **142–43**
pumping motion, **139**–41
slide-into-the-carve drill, **36**
Snowboarder, 7
snowboarding
acceptance of, xi–xiii
advances in, xii, 1, 3
as art, xiii, 3
individuality and personal
style, xiii, 64
learning, 1, 3–4
progression (progressive), 1,
3, 5
simplicity of, 3–4
Snowboard Magazine, 7
snowboards
choosing, 7
design elements, 7–12, **8**, **9**, **10**,
11
setup examples, **22–25**
technology advances, xii
types of, 7, **11–12**
Sorenson, Chauncy, **111**
stale fish, **50–51**, **114–15**
stance
importance of, 3, 17
learning, 4
setup examples, **22–25**
types of, 17–**21**
stance angles, 20–**21**
stance measurement, 20–**21**
Steward, Andrew "Droid", **23**, **47**,
48, **55**, **80**, **92**
straddle, **148**
stretching recommendations,
148–50
stump bonk, **90**, **91**
stump ollie, **83–84**, **90–91**
super pipe, 96
surfing, 97
switch, 20
switch indy, **56**

tables, 39, **43**. *See also* kickers
Tahoe City, 97
tail, **9**
tail bonk, **91**

tail butter, **133**–34
tail grab, **46–47**, **118–19**, **122–23**
tail kick, **8**
tail press, **92**
Thomas, J. J., **120**, **128**
tip, **9**
tip grabs, **128**, **129**
tip kick, **8**
toe ramp, **13**, 14
toe-side large-radius turn, **30–31**
toe-side medium-radius turn,
28–29
toe-side rail-grab drill, **37**, 98
toe-side wall, **96**
transitions (trannies)
location of, **96**, 97
pumping, 98, 99–100, **139**–41
TransWorld Snowboarding, 7
Troth, Jason, **47**, **133**
turns
board design for, 8, **9**
carving versus sliding, 26
drills, **36–37**, 98
elements of, 26–27
forward lean, **13**
importance of, 17
learning, 3
phases of, 26
types of, 26, **27–33**
twin-tip boards, **11–12**

up-flat-down log, **85**
up-flat-down rails, **78–79**
upper transition, **96**
vert, 96

warming up, 144
websites for gear research, 7
White, Shawn, **111**
width of boards, 8–9
Winterstick snowboard, xii
wood, sliding, 81. *See also* log
slides
wrist guards, 4
wrist injuries, 148
wrist stretches, **150**

Zaugg Pipe Monster, 96